Building a National Corpus

"The Welsh National Corpus is an important state-of-the-art corpus. Written with great precision and honesty, this book brings the reader inside the anatomy of the corpus and in doing so creates both an important archive of decision-making and protocols. Cutting-edge insights are also presented through case studies on spoken, written and e-language data from the corpus. For anyone attempting to build a corpus, this book is essential reading."

—Anne O'Keeffe, *University of Limerick, Ireland*

Dawn Knight · Steve Morris · Laura Arman ·
Jennifer Needs · Mair Rees

Building a National Corpus

A Welsh Language Case Study

Dawn Knight
School of English
Communication & Philosophy
Cardiff University
Cardiff, UK

Steve Morris
School of Culture and
Communication
Swansea University
Swansea, UK

Laura Arman
Wales Institute of Social and
Economic Research and Data
Cardiff University
Cardiff, UK

Jennifer Needs
Cardiff, UK

Mair Rees
Newport, UK

ISBN 978-3-030-81857-9 ISBN 978-3-030-81858-6 (eBook)
https://doi.org/10.1007/978-3-030-81858-6

© The Editor(s) (if applicable) and The Author(s), under exclusive licence to Springer
Nature Switzerland AG 2021
This work is subject to copyright. All rights are solely and exclusively licensed by the
Publisher, whether the whole or part of the material is concerned, specifically the rights
of translation, reprinting, reuse of illustrations, recitation, broadcasting, reproduction on
microfilms or in any other physical way, and transmission or information storage and
retrieval, electronic adaptation, computer software, or by similar or dissimilar methodology
now known or hereafter developed.
The use of general descriptive names, registered names, trademarks, service marks, etc.
in this publication does not imply, even in the absence of a specific statement, that such
names are exempt from the relevant protective laws and regulations and therefore free for
general use.
The publisher, the authors and the editors are safe to assume that the advice and information in this book are believed to be true and accurate at the date of publication. Neither
the publisher nor the authors or the editors give a warranty, expressed or implied, with
respect to the material contained herein or for any errors or omissions that may have been
made. The publisher remains neutral with regard to jurisdictional claims in published maps
and institutional affiliations.

Cover illustration: © Harvey Loake

This Palgrave Macmillan imprint is published by the registered company Springer Nature
Switzerland AG
The registered company address is: Gewerbestrasse 11, 6330 Cham, Switzerland

Preface

It is estimated that half of the world's population speak one of twenty-three languages (Eberhard et al., 2020). These twenty-three languages, which include, for example, English and Spanish, are generally well-resourced. They possess, among other resources, substantial and varied language corpora. These corpora are used to inform corpus and acquisition planning (concepts typically used in language planning research, e.g. Cooper, 2010), pedagogy and language technology development, enabling speakers of these languages to, for example, engage with their personal devices using their own voices, command their television sets to search for specific programmes or enable their PCs to transcribe their speech into written form. This book focuses on building national corpora mainly (but not exclusively) for those languages which are spoken by the other 50% of the world's population.

This book's prime focus is on how a circa 11-million-word corpus of contemporary Welsh was built and how this process can help inform those working with other languages to apply/adapt the methodology to their own needs. The book provides a micro-level, working model of a methodological approach to, and practical guidelines for, building a corpus informed by the work on the CorCenCC project (Corpws Cenedlaethol Cymraeg Cyfoes—The National Corpus of Contemporary Welsh). It is hoped that through sharing this approach to corpus building in Welsh and some of the unique challenges faced, others might be encouraged to attempt similar projects to develop resources in, and maintain the health and vitality of, their own language contexts and communities.

There is not one overarching template for building a corpus that will fit all languages. Similarly, the resources and approaches used to create corpora in larger and/or well-resourced languages are often not available or wholly relevant to corpus building in what might be termed under-resourced, minority, minoritised, non-dominant or lesser-used languages. Nevertheless, the path to creating CorCenCC is one that others may wish to follow or adapt to meet the challenges of embarking on similar corpus building projects for their own language communities.

REFERENCES

Cooper, R. L. (2010). *Language planning and social change.* Cambridge University Press.

Eberhard, D. M., Simons, G. F., & Fennig, C. D. (2020). *Ethnologue: Languages of the World. Twenty-third edition [Online].* Retrieved from http://www.eth nologue.com. Accessed 20 June 2021.

ACKNOWLEDGEMENTS

The research on which this book is based was funded by the UK Economic and Social Research Council (ESRC) and Arts and Humanities Research Council (AHRC) as part of the *Corpws Cenedlaethol Cymraeg Cyfoes (The National Corpus of Contemporary Welsh): A community driven approach to linguistic corpus construction* project (Grant Number ES/M011348/1). Thanks must also be given to former members and volunteers on the project's Work Package 1 (WP1) team who helped to collect and collate the data in CorCenCC, including: Laurence Anthony, Jeremy Evas, Tesni Galvin, Alys Greene, Sioned Johnson-Dowdeswell, Alex Lovell, Jonathan Morris, Mark Stonelake, Bethan Tovey-Walsh, Gareth Watkins, Lowri Williams, Lowri Williams, Katharine Young. The authors of this book would also like to acknowledge the extended CorCenCC team and its Co-Investigators (CIs), Research Assistants (RAs), consultants, stakeholders, ambassadors, as well as all data contributors and transcribers, without whom the project, and building the corpus, would not have been possible.

CONTENTS

1 Understanding the Language Context	1
Overview and Aims	2
National Corpora	5
Language Context: Key Definitions	8
Welsh-Language Corpora	14
Contextualising CorCenCC	17
References	19
2 Design Frames	23
General Principles	23
Spoken Corpora	28
Spoken Contexts	33
Public/Institutional	36
Media	38
Transactional	40
Professional	41
Pedagogic	42
Socialising and Private	44
Written Corpora	46
Size and Sampling	47
Sampling and Categorising Written Welsh	49
Defining e-Language	55
Genres of e-Language	56
E-Language Corpora	58

	Piloting Corpus Building	61
	Sampling and Categorising Welsh e-Language	63
	Summary	68
	References	68

3	**(Meta)Data Collection**	75
	Overviews	75
	Participant Recruitment	76
	Data Collection	78
	Metadata	84
	Demographic Targets: Spoken	92
	Copyright, Permissions and Ethics	95
	References	100

4	**Processing and (Re)presenting Corpora**	105
	Overview	105
	Transcribing Spoken Data	106
	Automated Anonymisation and Suitability Tagging	114
	Tagging	117
	Corpus Management Software	120
	Y Tiwtiadur	130
	References	133

5	**Results, Reflections and Lessons Learnt**	137
	Overview	137
	Spoken Data in CorCenCC	138
	Reflections and Lessons Learnt I	149
	Written Data in CorCenCC	152
	Reflections and Lessons Learnt II	158
	E-Language Data in CorCenCC	160
	Reflections and Lessons Learnt III	164
	Concluding Remarks	166
	References	168

Appendices	171
Index	181

LIST OF FIGURES

Fig. 1.1	Key stages of corpus building explored in this book	5
Fig. 2.1	Workflow for creating corpus design frames	68
Fig. 3.1	Promotional coaster used to recruit contributors to the CorCenCC corpus	77
Fig. 4.1	Workflow for transcribing spoken corpora	112
Fig. 4.2	User login options in CorCenCC's database management tool	121
Fig. 4.3	Examples of CorCenCC Data Management Tool interfaces	122
Fig. 4.4	KWIC output for '*dydd*' in CorCenCC (30 random instances from 11,057)	125
Fig. 4.5	Word identifier functionality in CorCenCC's *Y Tiwtiadur*	132
Fig. 5.1	CorCenCC's spoken demographics compared to the 2011 census (ONS, 2011)	147

LIST OF TABLES

Table 1.1	Selected under-resourced language corpora and corpus projects	12
Table 2.1	Original broad design frame for CorCenCC	26
Table 2.2	Design frame for spoken 'public/institutional' contexts in CorCenCC	37
Table 2.3	Design frame for spoken 'media' contexts in CorCenCC	39
Table 2.4	Design frame for spoken 'transactional' contexts in CorCenCC	41
Table 2.5	Design frame for spoken 'professional' contexts in CorCenCC	42
Table 2.6	Design frame for spoken 'pedagogic' contexts in CorCenCC	43
Table 2.7	Design frame for spoken 'socialising' contexts in CorCenCC	45
Table 2.8	Design frame for spoken 'private' contexts in CorCenCC	45
Table 2.9	Design frame for books in CorCenCC	50
Table 2.10	Design frame for magazines, newspapers and journals in CorCenCC	54
Table 2.11	Design frame for miscellaneous written data in CorCenCC	55
Table 2.12	Design frame for e-language data in CorCenCC	67
Table 3.1	Welsh speakers in each of local authorities in Wales (ONS, 2011)	93
Table 4.1	Top 20 most frequent words in CorCenCC (across all modes)	127

xiv   LIST OF TABLES

Table 4.2	Collocates of '*gyfer*' at $n-/+1$, listed according to the frequency of co-occurrence	130
Table 5.1	Composition of CorCenCC's spoken sub-corpus	140
Table 5.2	Genres in the CorCenCC's spoken 'broadcast' data	142
Table 5.3	Composition of CorCenCC's spoken 'educational' data	144
Table 5.4	Breakdown of the 'social' data in CorCenCC	145
Table 5.5	Breakdown of the 'private' data in CorCenCC	146
Table 5.6	Location of spoken data contributors ($n = 515$: 298 contributors did not provide this information)	147
Table 5.7	Comparing CorCenCC's written sub-corpus design frame with the final sub-corpus	153
Table 5.8	CorCenCC's written sub-corpus composition (with revised categorisations)	154
Table 5.9	Composition of the e-language sub-corpus in CorCenCC	161
Table 5.10	Website and blog topics of CorCenCC's e-language sub-corpus	161

CHAPTER 1

Understanding the Language Context

Abstract The book aims to provide a micro-level, working model of a methodological approach to, and practical guidelines for, building a corpus informed by the work on the CorCenCC project. This first chapter provides the context to the work and lays foundations for the first step of corpus building, that is, the examination of the context of the language. It begins with an exploration of what can be considered distinct about a 'national' corpus, and then examines how context affects the nature of a national corpus, including the differences between national corpora of major languages (both well-resourced and under-resourced) and those in under-resourced and/or minoritised languages. Following these discussions, the chapter overviews some existing language corpora created in under-resourced languages and explains the status of the Welsh language within this landscape.

Keywords Under-resourced language · Minority language · Minoritised language · Non-dominant language · Lesser-used language · National corpora · Sociolinguistic audit · Language context

© The Author(s), under exclusive license to Springer Nature
Switzerland AG 2021
D. Knight et al., *Building a National Corpus*,
https://doi.org/10.1007/978-3-030-81858-6_1

Overview and Aims

Given the increasing importance, wide utility and applications of corpora and corpus-based methods, there is a growing realisation that the creation of language resources, including corpora and corpus tools, is vital in sustaining and developing what are often described as under-resourced, minority, minoritised, non-dominant or lesser-used languages (i.e. typically those languages outside of the twenty-three spoken by half the world's population referred to in the foreword). The European Language Resources Association (ELRA—www.elra.info/en), for example, established a workshop series dedicated to Less-Resourced Languages (LRL), as well as a Special Interest Group for Under-resourced Languages (SIGUL), in collaboration with the International Speech Communication Association (ISCA—www.isca-speech.org). There are also an increasing number of research projects (including the Digital Language Diversity Project—www.dldp.eu) and academic conferences being held that focus on this topic, and numerous academic articles have been published on this in a range of computational, engineering, linguistics and other journals (e.g.Besacier et al., 2014; El-Haj et al., 2015; Scannell, 2007).

This book focuses on building national corpora mainly (but not exclusively) for under-resourced languages. It discusses, specifically, the creation of a corpus in the Welsh-language context: CorCenCC (*Corpws Cenedlaethol Cymraeg Cyfoes*—the National Corpus of Contemporary Welsh). Although Welsh is the language under discussion here, the aim is that sharing the experience of building CorCenCC through this book will enable many of the processes and approaches discussed to be applied to a lesser or greater extent to other language contexts. Wales is a bilingual country where the 2011 census (Welsh Government, 2012) recorded 562,016 speakers of Welsh (19% of the population of Wales) with varying geographical densities, age profiles, acquisition trajectories and reading and writing skills (ONS, 2011). CorCenCC is the first large-scale contemporary corpus of Welsh to account for these variations, capturing language usage across communication modes (spoken, written, e-language), genres, language varieties (regional and social) and contexts.

CorCenCC was 'user-driven' (Knight et al., 2021: 44–53) in its design, engaging closely with contemporary users of Welsh in the composition and promotion of the resource. This engagement with the users of Welsh was fundamental in ensuring that the end product was relevant to the language community and accurately reflected its contemporary constituency. The corpus, which was released in November 2020 (available at: www.corcencc.org), provides a resource to enhance and facilitate corpus and acquisition planning in Wales through, for example, supporting language technology (speech recognition, predictive text, etc.) and lexicography as well as pedagogical and academic research.

A description of the main objectives and achievements of the wider CorCenCC project is available in the final project report (Knight et al., 2020). Building on this, Knight et al. 2021 provide a rationale for, and realisation of the wider CorCenCC project (across all areas of activity). They present the conceptual framework for the user-driven design that underpinned the project, offering a blueprint for other researchers embarking on projects of this nature.

Complementing Knight et al. 2021's *conceptual framework*, this book is designed to be of significant value and relevance to those specifically interested in critically engaging with corpus building methodology. The book aims to provide a more *micro-level, working model of a methodological approach to, and practical guidelines for, building a corpus* informed by the work on the CorCenCC project. It focuses on the development of:

i. detailed design frames for corpora across communicative modes (spoken, written and e-language), and
ii. the practical processes involved in the planning, collection, transcription, collation and (re)presentation of language data.

It will become clear in the book that, to build a corpus, certain key elements need to be in place. In the case of CorCenCC, the project focused on five Work Packages (WPs) and organised the work through these. The WPs were interlinked and interdependent, collectively contributing to the realisation of the project's aims. The project team consisted of experts from corpus and applied linguistics, Welsh-language linguistics, pedagogy and computer science, from institutions in Wales, the rest of the UK and beyond. WP2 focused on the creation of a Welsh-language part-of-speech (POS) tagger and tagset; WP3 on a semantic tagger and tagset; WP4 on the development of a pedagogic toolkit and

WP5 on the creation of the corpus query tools and infrastructure for housing CorCenCC.

Reflections of the work carried out on WP1 are central to this book. The main objective of WP1 was to assemble a 10-million-word Welsh-language dataset (although as shown later, a figure of over 11-million-words was achieved). The key challenges/tasks associated with this objective were to:

1. create an appropriate design frame for the corpus
2. recruit potential participants/sources of data
3. collect written, spoken and e-language texts
4. design and apply transcription and anonymisation protocols to the data.

This book unpacks each of the challenges/tasks. It is our intention, through outlining the processes followed, and the decisions made in relation to each of these challenges/tasks, to provide guidance and a resource to other corpus and applied linguists who may be interested in building their own language corpus. To this end, this book is designed to provide:

i. a working model, and
ii. an account of building a corpus dataset, from which step-by-step guidelines for creating other linguistic corpora in *any* language can be easily extrapolated.

This first chapter provides the context to the work and lays foundations for the first step of corpus building, that is, the examination of the context of the language (using Welsh as a worked example of some of the things that need to be considered). It begins with an exploration of what can be considered distinct about a 'national' corpus, and then examines how context affects the nature of a national corpus, including the differences between national corpora of major languages (both well-resourced and under-resourced) and those in under-resourced and/or minoritised languages. Following these discussions, the chapter overviews some existing language corpora created in under-resourced languages and explains the status of the Welsh language within this landscape. Chapters 2, 3 and 4 detail some key stages of corpus building, illustrated in Fig. 1.1. This includes a focus on creating corpus design frames

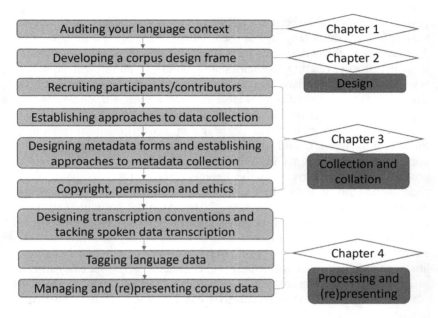

Fig. 1.1 Key stages of corpus building explored in this book

(Chapter 2), (meta)data collection and collation (Chapter 3) and data processing and (re)presentation (Chapter 4). While these chapters relate to the experiences of building CorCenCC, they aim to inform corpus building in other language contexts (including applicability to major languages).

Chapter 5 then examines to what extent the original plans for CorCenCC were realised and offers some reflections on the challenges faced when building the corpus, with practical advice on overcoming these.

National Corpora

So, what is a corpus? Broadly defined, a corpus (plural = corpora) is an electronic database of words. Corpora provide evidence of language as it is actually used in specific kinds of communication, by drawing on authentic examples, rather than on assumptions and beliefs: how individuals intuitively think language is used. Corpora are often annotated with grammatical information (i.e. POS—noun, verb, etc.) and/or semantic information (i.e. relating to themes and topics), in addition to metadata regarding where each language excerpt is from (e.g. genre, speaker location). This makes a corpus a valuable electronic tool as it allows users to explore and to better understand a given language.

'National' corpora are typically large in scale (i.e. multi-million or multi-billion words), and often, although not exclusively, contain a combination of written and spoken language (albeit typically a higher proportion of the former to the latter). That is, they are 'general' in their focus, and as they often aim to be 'representative of a particular national language variety' (Hawtin, 2018: 3), they contain texts from a range of different genres, contexts and/or speakers. Given the typical scale and scope (in terms of contents) of national corpora, these datasets are often used as reference corpora, that is, corpora that are used as a baseline against which more specialised (i.e. context or genre specific) and/or small-scale datasets are compared. These comparisons help to ascertain what is similar and/or different to what is 'expected' of a particular language or variety.

The 'first and best-known national corpus' (Xiao, 2008: 384) is the British National Corpus (BNC 1994 – Aston & Burnard, 1997). Built in the 1980s, the BNC 1994 extends to 100-million-words of written and spoken British English, at a distribution of 90 m: 10 m. The BNC 1994 has been used extensively in linguistic research, with a recent search of 'British National Corpus' on Google Scholar reportedly retrieving over 15,800 publications (Love, 2020: 13). A range of other 'national' corpora containing other varieties of English also exists, including those of American, Australian and Pakistani English, as well as 'national' corpora in other European (including Bulgarian, Croatian, Czech, Polish, Slovak, Hungarian, Croatian, Russian and Hellenic) and non-European (e.g. Nepali, Thai) languages. For an extensive list of mega and national corpora, see: http://martinweisser.org, Hawtin, 2018; Love, 2020).

A distinctive feature of 'national' corpora is that they represent language within, crudely speaking, prescribed geographical boundaries and/or political borders. When building a national corpus, decisions may need to be taken about what data within these boundaries/borders to include and exclude and why. The amount of material that might be available to be included in a national corpus will again vary according to the context of the language. Some minority languages such as the French language in Canada or a minoritised language such as Catalan have considerable governmental support and are far better resourced languages than, for example, most of UNESCO's 2500 languages in endangerment (see Moseley, 2010). Planning to build a national corpus would need to reflect the resources likely to be available for its construction and any possible constraints that might arise through this.

Careful consideration will, therefore, need to be given to the sociolinguistic and socio-political context of the language. A language might be used within some specific contexts and/or genres but hardly represented at all in others, for example in academic writing or in the legal system. The available data in some languages might be skewed towards spoken (or written) data and the corpus design would need to reflect this linguistic reality. Similarly, the presence of a language in the e-language mode might be healthy or it might not be very evident. Another important consideration would be the inclusion (or not) of e-language or written data that is predominantly formal and/or translated from a co-official major/majority language. A clear understanding of the contemporary sociolinguistic situation—a 'sociolinguistic audit'—of a language is therefore vital to undertake as the first stage of planning for any national corpus. The following are examples of the types of questions that might comprise part of this sociolinguistic audit, providing a baseline for defining your context:

- How many speakers of the language are there? Are they mainly bilingual or monolingual speakers?
- Where is the language spoken?
- Are other languages spoken within the same territory?
- What is the official status of the language?
- How well-resourced is the language?
- Are there any specific genres that do or do not exist in the language?
- Are there specific contexts in which the language is or is not used in?
- Is the language mainly spoken? Written? Digital?

- Is there a common demographic profile of a speaker of the language? E.g. age, gender, socio-economic background

The answers to these questions will impact on what is feasible to achieve when building a corpus in a given language context.

LANGUAGE CONTEXT: KEY DEFINITIONS

As already seen, there are many terms for describing languages that are not among the most widely spoken in the world including: under-resourced, minority, minoritised, lesser-used and/or non-dominant languages. It is useful to establish working definitions for these terms here. The term 'under-resourced', in reference to a language, is considered synonymous with the terms 'low density-languages, resource-poor languages, low-data languages, less-resourced languages' (Besacier et al., 2014: 87).

'Resources' might refer to access to basic services, learning materials (for reading, writing, language teaching), pedagogical materials (textbooks and curricula), online opportunities for the language or any combination of these. The absence of these may result in speakers (or users) of that language being at a disadvantage in their educational or cultural experiences. When languages are under-resourced, the population that uses the language exclusively is either somehow linguistically impoverished or forced to acquire an additional language to gain access to the same level of socio-economic status through education or opportunity.

An under-resourced language is 'not the same as a minority language [...] some under-resourced languages are actually official languages of their country and spoken by a very large population' (Besacier et al., 2014). A 'minority' language can refer to languages spoken by a minority of the population or whose status is lower than the 'majority' language. A 'majority language', in contrast, can be broadly defined as one that is spoken by most of a population (in a given country or region) and used as the basis for daily communication in most domains, for example, work, education, the media and the law. While under-resourcing is often associated with minority/minoritised languages, it should be noted that for historical and socio-economic reasons, even some widely spoken 'majority' languages might be under-resourced in some contexts. For example, speakers of European Portuguese can only access the Brazilian variety through Apple's voice assistant Siri even though English and Spanish speakers can access several varieties of their languages. In terms of technological resources, only a few of the world's languages 'enjoy the benefits of modern language technologies such as speech recognition and machine translation' (Scannell, 2007: 1). While this landscape may have changed in the past 13 years, there is still a gulf in the resources available to the various languages of the world.

The focus of this book—Welsh—is representative of a 'minoritised language', which can be defined in the context of historical socioeconomic conditions as well as the resulting psychological mechanisms imposed upon it (Hinton et al., 2018). This is a more apposite term for the purposes of highlighting the resources (or lack thereof) available and attitudes ascribed to a language's users, than labels such as 'minority' or 'lesser-used'. ELEN (the European Language Equality Network—https://elen.ngo/information/) defines 'lesser-used' as including regional, minority, endangered, indigenous, co-official and smaller national languages. An alternative term is RML (Regional, Minority or Endangered Language). While these terms would apply to a language such as Welsh, these terms are not necessarily applicable to all under-resourced languages.

The definition of the term 'minoritised' itself can be interpreted broadly or narrowly (see Knight et al., 2021: 6–10). In the context of this book, this term is not always interchangeable with a 'minority' language. 'Minoritised' refers to the present-day attitudes, use and resources of a language due to historical factors. Some minoritised languages located in more affluent areas of the world (e.g. Europe) have succeeded in attracting a certain degree of corpus and language planning resource through devolved political institutions and being a focus for academic research. However, many minoritised languages are typically also under-resourced ones, due to an imbalance in the demand for and the rate of development (often technological) of these resources.

The terms 'dominant language' and 'non-dominant language' are preferred by some as an alternative to the majority/minority language divide (e.g. Benson, 2014). The official status of a language and its speaker population size are not the sole determiner of whether 'resources' will be available to its speakers, particularly if historically the language has been subjugated by another more politically dominant one. South Africa, for example, has eleven official languages, but they do not all have access to equal resources. When a minoritised language in a bilingual context is under-resourced, it is therefore more susceptible to language shift, especially in smaller population sizes, as its speakers have a stronger incentive to make use of the other well-resourced language. This book focuses primarily on building a language resource (a corpus) in under-resourced contexts.

To enable equitable opportunities so as not to place one language community at a disadvantage compared to another, a minimum level of linguistic resources should be available:

- a way of preserving linguistic knowledge (an orthography, a dictionary, a basic descriptive grammar), and
- a sustainable way of developing new resources (a large enough quantity of linguistic data for the language to be studied further and to serve as exemplars for as many contexts as possible).

Building corpora answers the second need here: a corpus provides a verifiable source of linguistic data in a format that can be repurposed to develop further resources.

Scannell (2007), a key figure in developing corpus resources for under-resourced languages, points out that building large corpora is expensive, and tends to be subject to market pressures that favour the languages with most potential users. Efforts to create corpora for under-resourced languages must come from non-market-driven sources, i.e. non-commercial enterprises, such as government-funded research councils, personal volunteer projects and so on.

There are two basic ways to get a corpus for an under-resourced language off the ground. One is to obtain sufficient funding to create it from scratch. However, access to such funding is competitive and there is no guarantee that financial support will be forthcoming. It is nevertheless vital for the development of a linguistic corpus, an activity that 'arguably involves a greater investment of time, resources and energy than any other type of linguistic activity' (Beal et al., 2007: ix). The other way is to piggyback on the infrastructure of existing corpora for well-resourced languages and replicate/extend their tools and resources for use in the target language context, rather than reinvent them. Several projects have sought to facilitate the creation of corpora of under-resourced, minority, minoritised, non-dominant or lesser-used languages, that is, to provide

1 UNDERSTANDING THE LANGUAGE CONTEXT 11

the basic tools required to build a corpus so these languages can benefit from corpora in the same way that major languages already do. Scannell's An Crúbadán project is an example of this. It has built over 2000 large web-scraped corpora for a variety of languages, including Welsh (Scannell, 2007). Another example is the CorpusBuilder tool, 'an approach for automatically generating web-search queries for collecting documents in a minority language' (Ghani et al., 2005: 56).

Similarly, the developers of the (now widely used) Sketch Engine tool aimed to create a 'corpus factory' with the primary goal of making 'the task of corpora collection easy with minimal or no human intervention' (Kilgarriff et al., 2010: 1). This facility lends itself in particular to under-resourced languages and has been used in the creation of corpora in Afrikaans, Catalan, Limburgish, Frisian, Maori, Breton among others. Sketch Engine currently includes corpora in over 90 languages (including majority and minority/minoritised, under-resourced languages and so on: https://www.sketchengine.eu/corpora-and-languages/). Further examples of selected language corpora created for under-resourced languages (beyond those featured in Sketch Engine) are documented in Table 1.1.

A challenge encountered when building a corpus of such languages is the ability to build datasets that include, for example, a range of genres and text types, and a balance of sociolinguistic variables (if spoken), as they just may not exist (see discussions of the 'sociolinguistic audit' above). Similarly, individuals with the appropriate linguistic expertise to undertake such a project may not exist. Yadava et al., for example, replicated the basic design of the English-language Brown family corpora (principally the Freiburg-LOB corpus, Hundt et al., 1998, also see Chapter 2) in their corpus of Nepalese, but modifications to the design frame had to be made because 'not all the genres that can be identified in English actually exist in Nepali' (2008: 215). While, when building the corpus of Banat Czech (a Czech minority language spoken in 6 villages in the Romanian Banat region), it wasn't possible to balance variables of age and gender in the dataset as 'most speakers are women aged over fifty' and shared the same demographic profile (Vyskočilová, 2016: 157).

Further to this, technological approaches commonly employed for data collection, such as OCR (Optical Character Recognition), as used in the original BNC 1994, do not work for many under-resourced language contexts, including some of those represented by the corpora listed in Table 1.1. OCR is where handwritten or printed text documents are scanned and converted into digital characters. OCR requires extensive

Table 1.1 Selected under-resourced language corpora and corpus projects

Corpus and/or reference	Language	Details
AsoSoft Text Corpus, Mohammadamini et al. (2019)	Kurdish	190-million-tokens from 458,000 texts including websites, books, and magazines, in TEI format (Text Encoding Initiative, see Chapter 4)
Corpas na Gaeilge Comhaimseartha (Corpus of Contemporary Irish), Ní Loingsigh et al. (2017)	Irish	14.9-million-word unannotated corpus of digital texts. This includes, for example, blogs, social media texts and fiction and non-fiction from 2000 onwards
Corpus of Basque Simplified Texts (CBST), Gonzalez-Dios et al. (2018)	Basque	Corpus of simplified texts comprising 227 original sentences from the domain of popularised science and two simplified versions of each sentence
Corpus Oral Informatizado, da Lingua Galega (CORILGA), García-Mateo et al. (2014)	Galician	98 h of audio recordings with corresponding annotated orthographic transcriptions. Includes a range of genres including talks, broadcast interviews, TV shows and literary readings. This project also built a software repository for Galician speech resources
CUCWeb, Boleda et al. (2006)	Catalan	166-million-word corpus of annotated web-crawled texts
DigiSami, Jokinen (2018)	North Sami	257 min of unannotated read speech data and 195 min of annotated data, including speakers aged 16–65. Created as part of the SamiTalk project which developed spoken/speech technologies for North Sami
Korpus Malti v3.0, Gatt and Čéplö (2013)	Maltese	250-million-token written corpus with texts from various genres. POS/morphologically tagged and lemmatised

Corpus and/or reference	Language	Details
Nepali National Corpus (NNC), Yadava et al. (2008)	Nepali	14-million-word corpus of spoken and written texts in the Devanagari script. There are two separate written corpora: Nepal-English and English-Nepal
Nua-Chorpas na hÉireann (New Corpus for Ireland—NCI). Kilgarriff et al. (2006)	Irish	30-million-word part-of-speech (POS) tagged written corpus. Created to enable the development of an English-Irish Dictionary. Funded by *Foras na Gaeilge*, a public body responsible for promoting the Irish language
Ossetic National Corpus (ONS), Arkhangelskiy et al. (2012)	Ossetic	12-million-token corpus. 2/3 of the corpus comprise texts from the literary journal *Makh dug*, along with texts from online newspapers, fiction, and poetry from 1996–2014
Scottish Corpus of Texts and Speech (SCOTS), Anderson et al. (2007)	Scots	4.6-million-word corpus comprising text and audio recordings (with their orthographic transcriptions), accompanied by detailed metadata information, and presented as an online multimodal resource
The Corpus of Greek Texts, Goutsos (2010)	Cypriot Greek	30-million-word general/reference monolingual corpus of written and spoken Greek, collected over two decades
Vyskočilová (2016)	Banat Czech	200,000 word spoken corpus from 20 local informants (mainly women in their 50s)
Wibawa et al. (2018)	Javanese and Sudanese	Crowdsourced collection of 5800 Javanese and 4200 Sudanese mixed-gender recordings, to facilitate the development of text-to-speech systems

manual input, in both scanning and checking, but this is arguably still easier and quicker than keying in characters by hand. This approach proved inoperable, for example, for all of the languages included in the EMILLE project (Enabling Minority Language Engineering, Baker et al., 2004). EMILLE developed 14 corpora of 1.64+ million words for under-resourced Indic languages (97-million-words in total) including Tamil, Hindi, Singhalese, Punjabi, Urdu, Gujarati, and Bengali. In consequence, any written data used was required to be machine-readable, internet-based, and extracted by the project team (manually, not automatically).

Issues relating to the lack of transcription, coding and/or annotation coding conventions (and tools) are also sometimes encountered in under-resourced language contexts, often requiring researchers to develop their own (which was partly the case with the Welsh-language context and CorCenCC itself). Again, the EMILLE project, which also aimed to capture spoken discourse, experienced further challenges with language attitudes and prescriptivism pertaining to the spoken form of some languages. Speakers of the languages were recruited as transcribers and were asked to transcribe the language of the recordings as they heard it. In the case of Hindi, for example, this 'caused some transcribers who happily worked on typing parallel corpus data to refuse to work' with the spoken materials as there was a common belief that people should use 'classical Hindi texts and not the bastardised slang' (Baker et al., 2004: 516). This challenge confirmed that attitudes towards language as a linguist and as a user of a language are not necessarily one and the same. This is a problem that needs careful consideration when embarking on building language corpora as it is unlikely to be unique to the EMILLE project. Further challenges and considerations for corpus building are explored in Chapters 2, 3 and 4.

Welsh-Language Corpora

As a minoritised language in the UK context (although having official and therefore legal status in Wales–Welsh Language Measure, WLWM, 2011), Welsh has not enjoyed the same corpus resources as English or other major state languages. Nevertheless, a number of attempts have been made over the years to create Welsh-language corpora (for a full discussion and list of these, see Knight et al., 2021: 25–27). Not all these corpora are equipped with integrated online search and query tools, that is, as some require users to access the data online and search it using their own tools. The availability of the data also varies from corpus to corpus, ranging from those that are completely open and available to download and search, to those that are available but are difficult to search and, finally, to corpora whose data is unavailable for users to access directly but the analysis of certain features is mapped out online. The variation is due to both the purpose of the corpus and the design of its online interface, and restrictions imposed by usage rights and data.

The existing Welsh corpora fall into five main types:

1. Small corpora (<1-million-words) of spoken data transcribed for linguistic research. Examples include: Aberystwyth Child Language Databases: CIG1 and CIG2 (Jones, 1996, 2000), Patagonia corpus of Welsh-Spanish bilingual speech (Deuchar, 2011) and *Siarad* (Deuchar et al., 2018)
2. Crowdsourced recordings of spoken data for the purposes of speech recognition. Examples include: *Paldaruo* Speech Corpus (Cooper et al., 2019) and Mozilla Common Voice (https://voice.mozilla.org/)
3. Parallel bilingual corpora of edited written language. Examples include: *Kynulliad3* (Donnelly, 2013) and UAGT-PNAW Parallel Welsh-English Corpus (Jones & Eisele, 2006)
4. Corpora of written and edited texts from published works. Examples include: *Cronfa Electroneg o Gymraeg* (CEG—Ellis et al., 2001), DECHE Corpus of Welsh Scholarly Writing (Prys et al., 2014) and *Ein Geiriau Ni*—Corpus of Children's Literature in Welsh (NFER, 2005)
5. Large corpora of texts scraped from online sources, including social media. Examples include: *Trydarieitheg*/Tweetolectology (Willis et al., 2019), Corpus of Facebook Welsh Language Texts (Jones et al., 2015), *Crúbadán*—Welsh Corpus (Scannell, 2007), Korrect (Donnelly, 2014a) and Kwici corpus (Donnelly, 2014b).

Natural speech corpora (i.e. type 1 above) prioritise creating a record of the language for current and future research, and the transcription necessarily incorporates annotations relevant to that purpose, but which are not particularly useful for other applications such as improving machine learning. The *Siarad* corpus (a 460 k word spoken corpus comprising transcriptions of 40 h of conversations between 151 speakers from different parts of Wales, Deuchar et al., 2018), however, provides the original recordings together with a rich set of metadata alongside the transcribed texts. This means that the data from *Siarad* can be used in additional advantageous ways, such as training forced aligners and so on.

The corpora that were designed with a focus on improving machine learning are generally larger than other Welsh-language corpora because the material is collected through automated processes from the web. The accuracy and quality of these datasets are dependent on how carefully the researchers constructed their method to identify Welsh texts and how much they were able to edit their corpus after scraping to remove any undesired results.

As mentioned above, some of the existing corpora come with their own query interfaces. However, since they are designed to fulfil certain functions or to answer specific questions, they are not always open to broader application. For example, an end user wishing to search for grammatical features such as specific suffixes might find that there is no mechanism for doing so. Such design limitations restrict the potential for both research and pedagogical purposes. In consequence, while a wealth of linguistic data has been collected, it is not always accessible to those who wish to exploit it for the benefit of a variety of different applications, such as for the development of speech recognition and speech-to-text utilities. An additional disadvantage is the unavailability of the original raw data in many instances, especially in large datasets. This is usually due to legal permissions and intellectual property rights—what is convenient to collect is not always available to share publicly.

Similar situations may exist in other language contexts, particularly where specialised corpora have been compiled. It is clearly always advisable to scope what has been produced previously, and to determine for what purpose they have been produced, to identify resource gaps that exist. These gaps can be addressed in future corpus building projects.

A major lacuna in the set of Welsh corpora before CorCenCC was any sizeable corpus representing contemporary Welsh-language use in different contexts. Some of the corpora include specific modes of data and/or genres of text, such as CIG1 which contains child language (conversations between children ages 18 and 30 months, Jones, 1996) and DECHE (currently 30 books, circa 450,000 words, Prys et al., 2014), which contains one genre of text (i.e. scholarly writing). Both corpora are, to an extent, controlled by demographics—i.e. by age and by socio-economic background (they are academic texts). The scraped web corpora, on the other hand, beg the question 'whose Welsh is this?' as the web-scraping facilities do not allow for careful selection by user (see Chapter 3 for an explanation of web-scraping). A possible exception is corpora comprised of web-scraped microblogging sites where specific users are tagged. Even then, connecting those users to their demographic background involves time-consuming research that many developers of this type of corpus have not carried out. *Trydarieitheg*/Tweetolectology is a corpus that attempts to overcome this shortcoming, as it has a particular interest in user demographics along with geographical variants. *Trydarieitheg*/Tweetolectology comprises a group of corpora scraped from Twitter, including a Welsh corpus comprised of all Tweets found in Welsh and dated from December 2017–December 2019 (1.86 million Tweets). The project aimed to track the diffusion of certain grammatical features throughout the population and has developed a method of determining its users' location and origin to map this geographical spread (Willis et al., 2019). Unfortunately, at the time of publication, the source of their data prohibits its publication online so it cannot be used by others.

Contextualising CorCenCC

CorCenCC is the first large-scale corpus of naturally occurring real-life Welsh-language use that endeavours to represent the diversity of contemporary Welsh speakers, as well as reflecting the wide range of contexts in which they use the language. That is, its aim is to provide a *general, national* corpus, one that includes data sampled from a range of speakers (of different ages, genders and occupations), across a range of different discourse contexts, and geographical locations in Wales. This composition enables users to make generalised observations about language use (i.e. not restricted to a specific discourse context or domain) and to undertake enquiries of the data directed by their own interests and requirements.

CorCenCC is designed to provide users of Welsh with a clear and principled snapshot of language use today, offering evidence to challenge preconceptions about the language and a databank to facilitate the development of social, educational and technological resources. Recent Welsh Government policy proposes to increase the number of Welsh speakers in Wales to one million by 2050. CorCenCC has an important role to play in the work programme for phase 2017–2021, which envisages support for the 'the production of more high-quality lexicographical, corpus and terminology resources to support learners and fluent speakers' (Welsh Government, 2017: 27). CorCenCC is a model for those keen to protect and build capacity in their own language (see Knight et al., 2021: 44–53, 70–75 for a more detailed discussion of the potential uses and audiences of CorCenCC).

The questions that can be asked of a corpus, and the relative 'value' that is provided by one are dependent on the specific nature and composition of the resource: on the data that has been captured within it. This leads on to the rest of this volume: to provide a practical account of how the CorCenCC resource was built.

'The principles of building a corpus of a major national language and of a small understudied language are different' (Vinogradov, 2016: 128). This is due to the resource-related challenges discussed above, and the possible lack of availability of relevant text material, among other factors. This does not mean, however, that common approaches to corpus composition in well-resourced languages cannot offer useful guidelines for building a corpus in an under-resourced/minoritised language context. While there have been calls for standardisation in corpus building, this has yet to be achieved. This is owing to the fact that corpora are built to fulfil a specific purpose/use, the requirements for which have a direct impact on what goes into the dataset and which specific approaches are employed to build it. While there is a lack of *standard* practices, there are some *shared* practices that provide a useful point of departure for undertaking corpus projects. A natural starting point for building a corpus is to examine previous work in predominantly well-resourced language contexts and adapt the approaches to, and requirements for, its own context. This on-going examination is central to this book.

This begins, in Chapter 2, with a detailed discussion of what a corpus design frame is and demonstrates how design frames might be developed to guide corpus building. While these discussions are contextualised with reference to the CorCenCC project and specifically, they serve as the second stage of our practical 'how-to' for building a corpus, that may, again, be applied to *any language*.

REFERENCES

Anderson, J., Beavan, D., & Kay, C. (2007). SCOTS: Scottish corpus of texts and speech. In J. Beal, K. Corrigan, & H. Moisl (Eds.), *Creating and digitizing language corpora: Volume 1—synchronic databases* (pp. 17–34). Palgrave Macmillan.

Arkhangelskiy, T., Belyaev, O., & Vydrin, A. (2012). The creation of large-scaled annotated corpora of minority languages using UniParser and the EANC platform. In *Proceedings of the International Conference on Computational Linguistics (COLING)* (pp. 83–91). Mumbai.

Aston, G., & Burnard, L. (1997). *The BNC Handbook: Exploring the British National Corpus with SARA*. Edinburgh: Edinburgh University Press.

Baker, P., Hardie, A., McEnery, T., Xiao, R., Bontcheva, K., Cunningham, H., Gaizauskas, R., Hamza, O., Maynard, D., Tablan, V., Ursu, C., Jayaram, B. D., & Leisher, M. (2004). Corpus linguistics and south Asian languages: Corpus creation and tool development. *Literary and Linguistic Computing, 19*, 509–524.

Beal, J., Corrigan, K., & Moisl, H. (2007). *Creating and digitizing language corpora. Volume 1: Synchronic databases*. Palgrave Macmillan.

Benson, C. (2014). Adopting a multilingual habitus: What North and South can learn from each other about the essential role of non-dominant languages in education. In D. Gorter, V. Zenotz, & J. Cenoz (Eds.), *Minority languages and multilingual education* (pp. 11–28). Springer Netherlands.

Besacier, L., Barnard, E., Karpov, A., & Schultz, T. (2014). Automatic speech recognition for under-resourced languages: A survey. *Speech Communication, 56*, 85–100.

Boleda, G., Bott, S., Meza, R., Castillo, C., Badia, T., & López, V. (2006). CUCWeb: A Catalan corpus built from the web. In *Proceedings of the WAC'06 (2nd International Workshop on Web as Corpus)* (pp. 19–26). Bielefeld: Bielefeld University.

Cooper, S., Jones, D. B., & Prys, D. (2019). Crowdsourcing the Paldaruo speech corpus of Welsh for speech technology. *Information, 10*(8), 247–258.

Deuchar, M. (2011). *Patagonia corpus of Welsh-Spanish bilingual speech.* [Online]. http://www.bangortalk.org.uk/speakers.php?c=patagonia. Accessed 20 June 2021.

Deuchar, M., Webb-Davies, P., & Donnelly, K. (2018). *Building and using the Siarad Corpus*. John Benjamins.

Donnelly, K. (2013). *Kynulliad3: A corpus of 350,000 aligned Welsh and English sentences from the third Assembly (2007–2011) of the national assembly for Wales*. [Online]. http://cymraeg.org.uk/kynulliad3. Accessed 20 June 2021.

Donnelly, K. (2014a). *Korrect—a corpus of 43,000 aligned Welsh and English software translations*. [Online]. http://cymraeg.org.uk/korrect/. Accessed 20 June 2021.

20   D. KNIGHT ET AL.

Donnelly, K. (2014b). *Kwici: A 4m-word corpus drawn from the Welsh Wikipedia.* [Online]. http://cymraeg.org.uk/kwici. Accessed 20 June 2021.

El-Haj, M., Kruschwitz, U., & Fox, C. (2015). Creating language resources for under-resourced languages: Methodologies and experiments on Arabic. *Language Resources and Evaluation Journal, 49,* 549–580.

Ellis, N. C., O'Dochartaigh, C., Hicks, W., Morgan, M., & Laporte, N. (2001). *Cronfa Electroneg o Gymraeg (CEG): Cronfa ddata eirfaol, miliwn o eiriau, sy'n cyfrif amlder defnydd geiriau yn y Gymraeg.* [Online]. https://www.bangor.ac.uk/canolfanbedwyr/ceg.php.en. Accessed 20 June 2021..

García-Mateo, C., Cardenal, A., Regueira, X., Fernández Rei, E., Maquieira, M., Seara, R., Varela Fernández, R., & Basanta, N. (2014). CORILGA: A Galician multilevel annotated speech corpus for linguistic analysis. In *Proceedings of the Language Resources and Evaluation (LREC)* (pp. 2653–2657). Reykjavik, Iceland.

Gatt, A., & Čéplö, S. (2013). *Digital corpora and other electronic resources for Maltese.* Paper presented at the International Conference on Corpus Linguistics, Lancaster University, Lancaster.

Ghani, R., Jones, R., & Mladenic, D. (2005). Building minority language Corpora by learning to generate web search queries. *Knowledge and Information Systems, 7*(1), 56–83.

Gonzalez-Dios, I., Aranzabe, M. J., & Ilarraza, A. (2018). The corpus of Basque simplified texts (CBST). *Language Resources and Evaluation, 52,* 217–247.

Goutsos, D. (2010). The Corpus of Greek texts: A reference corpus for modern Greek. *Corpora, 5*(1), 29–44.

Hawtin, A. (2018). *The written British national corpus 2014: Design, compilation and analysis.*Unpublished Ph.D. Thesis, Lancaster University, Lancaster.

Hinton, L., Huss, L., & Roche, G. (Eds.). (2018). *The Routledge handbook of language revitalization.* Routledge.

Hundt, M., Sand, A., & Siemund, R. (1998). *Manual of information to accompany the Freiburgh-LOC Corpus of British English ('FLOB').* Albert-Ludwigs-Universität Freiburg.

Jokinen, K. (2018). Researching less-resourced languages—the DigiSami corpus. In *Proceedings of the Language Resources Evaluation Conference (LREC)* (pp. 3382–3386). Miyazaki, Japan.

Jones, B. M. (1996). *Aberystwyth child language databases: CIG1 [Online].* Retrieved from: http://users.aber.ac.uk/bmj/abercld/cronfa18_30/sae/intro.html. Accessed 20 June 2021.

Jones, B. M. (2000). *The Aberystwyth child language databases.* [Online]. http://users.aber.ac.uk/bmj/abercld/projects.html. Accessed 20 June 2021.

Jones, D., & Eisele, A. (2006). Phrase-based statistical machine translation between English and Welsh. In *Proceedings of the 5th SALTMIL workshop on*

Minority languages: Strategies for developing machine translation for minority languages (pp. 75–77). Genoa, Italy.

Jones, D. B., Robertson, P., & Taborda, A. (2015). *Corpus of Facebook Welsh language texts*. [Online]. http://techiaith.cymru/data/corpora/facebook/?lang=en. Accessed 20 June 2021.

Kilgarriff, A., Reddy, S., Pomikálek, J., & Pvs, A. (2010). A Corpus factory for many languages. In *Proceedings of the Language Resources and Evaluation (LREC)* (pp. 904–910).

Kilgarriff, A., Rundell, M., & Dhonnchadha, E. (2006). Efficient corpus development for lexicography: Building the new corpus for Ireland. *Language Resources and Evaluation, 40*, 127–152.

Knight, D., Morris, S., & Fitzpatrick, T. (2021). *Corpus design and construction in minoritised language contexts: The national corpus of contemporary Welsh*. Palgrave.

Knight, D., Morris, S., Fitzpatrick, T., Rayson, P., Spasić, I., & Môn Thomas, E. (2020). *The national corpus of contemporary Welsh: Project report | Y corpws cenedlaethol Cymraeg cyfoes: adroddiad y prosiect*. http://orca.cf.ac.uk/135540/. Accessed 20 June 2021.

Love, R. (2020). *Overcoming challenges in corpus construction*. Routledge.

Mohammadamini, M., Veisi, H., & Hosseini, H. (2019). Toward Kurdish language processing: Experiments in collecting and processing the AsoSoft text corpus, digital scholarship in the humanities. *Literary and Linguistic Computing, 35*(1), 176–193.

Moseley, C. (2010). *Atlas of the world's languages in danger* (3rd ed.). UNESCO Publishing.

NFER. (2005). *Ein Geiriau Ni—Corpus of children's literature in Welsh*. [Online]. https://www.egni.org/index.htm. Accessed 20 June 2021.

Ní Loingsigh, K., Raghallaigh, B., & Cléircín, G. (2017). *The Design and Development of Corpas na Gaeilge Comhaimseartha* [Corpus of Contemporary Irish]. Paper presented at the 9th International Corpus Linguistics Conference, University of Birmingham, UK.

ONS (Office for National Statistics). (2011). *Census: Digitised boundary data (England and Wales)*. [Computer File]. https://borders.ukdataservice.ac.uk/. Accessed 20 June 2021.

Prys, D., Jones, D., & Roberts, M. (2014). DECHE and the Welsh national corpus portal. In *Proceedings of the First Celtic Language Technology Workshop* (pp. 71–75).

Scannell, K. (2007). The Crúbadán project: Corpus building for under-resourced languages. *Cahiers Du Cental, 5*(1), 1–10.

Vinogradov, I. (2016). Linguistic corpora of understudied languages: Do they make sense? *Káñina, 40*(1), 127–141.

Vyskočilová, K. (2016). Czech language minority in the south-eastern Romanian Banat. *IJSL, 238*, 145–167.

Welsh Government. (2012). *A living language: A language for living: Welsh language strategy 2012–17*. [Online]. https://gov.wales/welsh-language-str ategy-2012-2017-living-language-language-living. Accessed 20 June 2021.

Welsh Government. (2017). *Cymraeg 2050: A million Welsh speakers Action Plan 2019–20*. [Online]. https://gov.wales/sites/default/files/publications/2019-03/cymraeg-2050-a-million-welsh-speakers-action-plan-2019-20.pdf. Accessed 20 June 2021.

Wibawa, J. A. E., Sarin, S., Li, C., Pipatsrisawat, K., Sodimana, K., Kjartansson, O., Gutkin, A., Jansche, M., & Ha, L. (2018). Building open Javanese and Sundanese corpora for multilingual text-to-speech. In *Proceedings of the Language resources and evaluation (LREC)* (pp. 1610–1614).

Willis, D., Gopal, D., Blaxter, T., & Leeman, A. (2019). *Tweetolectology*. [Online]. http://tweetolectology.com/index.html. Accessed 20 June 2021.

WLWM. (2011). *Welsh language (Wales) measure 2011*. http://www.legislation. gov.uk/mwa/2011/1/contents?lang=en. Accessed 20 June 2021.

Xiao, R. (2008). Well-known and influential corpora. In A. Lüdeling & M. Kytö (Eds.), *Corpus linguistics: An international handbook* (Vol. 1, pp. 383–456). Walter de Gruyter.

Yadava, Y. P., Hardie, A., Lohani, R. R., Regmi, B. H., Gurung, S., Gurung, A., McEnery, T., Allwood, J., & Hall, P. (2008). Construction and annotation of a corpus of contemporary Nepali. *Corpora, 3*(2), 213–225.

CHAPTER 2

Design Frames

Abstract Using a case study approach, this chapter provides a worked demonstration of how a detailed design frame for a national corpus may be built. Focusing on each individual 'mode' of data in turn (i.e. spoken, written and e-language), the chapter explores some key generic questions that are helpful in informing design frame development. By reporting on the specific targets presented, and providing justifications for these, useful guidance for those considering creating their own corpus design frame emerges. While the points raised in this chapter relate to our experiences of creating design frames for CorCenCC specifically, the guidance provided can facilitate and inform the design of corpora in other languages.

Keywords Design frame · Mode · Genre · Context · Representativeness · Balance · Text types · Topic · Sample size · Taxonomies · Pilot study

GENERAL PRINCIPLES

In Chapter 1, a basic definition of a corpus as 'an electronic database of words' was given. This definition can be usefully extended, as follows (Gries & Newman, 2014: 258):

© The Author(s), under exclusive license to Springer Nature Switzerland AG 2021
D. Knight et al., *Building a National Corpus*,
https://doi.org/10.1007/978-3-030-81858-6_2

23

The prototypical corpus is a *machine-readable* collection of language used in authentic settings/contexts: that is intended to be *representative* for a particular, language variety, or register (in the sense of reflecting all the possible parts of the intended language/variety/register) and that is intended to be *balanced* such that the sizes of the parts of the corpus correspond to the proportion these parts make up in the language/variety/register.

Corpora may contain a range of different genres/text-types (i.e. a *balance*), and while it is technically possible to collect the entire 'population' of some language types and/or varieties (e.g. in specialist corpora dedicated to the works of a particular author), when building general and national corpora, even in many minority/minoritised contexts, this is not feasible. Typically, only a *representative* snapshot/sample of the overall linguistic variety or population can be collected.

Decisions regarding what types of data and how much are to be collected at a genre and/or text level are ultimately underpinned by which of the two umbrella approaches to corpus building is used. These are the 'monitor' approach (Sinclair, 1991: 24–26) and the 'balanced or sample' approach (Biber, 1994). 'Monitor' corpora are those that are not static/fixed in size and continue to grow over time, such as the 310-million-word French language CRFC corpus (Siepmann et al., 2015). Corpora built using the balanced/sample approach, instead, provide a snapshot of language use at a fixed/given point in time (i.e. they are static in size). Examples of balanced/sample-based corpora include the original BNC 1994 and the Written BNC2014. COCA (Davies, 2010) combines both approaches: it continues to increase in size (aligning to the monitor approach), with the addition of a 20% sample of each genre (i.e. spoken, fiction, popular magazines, newspapers and academic journals) to the corpus every year. As the CorCenCC project had a finite amount of time and resources available for building the corpus, the monitor approach was not initially applicable to its development. The balanced/sample approach was, instead, regarded as more appropriately aligned to CorCenCC's aims of capturing a representative *sample* of Welsh language as it is currently used and encountered.

Regarding size, while there are large-scale corpora in existence, it is not necessarily the case that 'the bigger the corpus the better'. On a practical level, 'the question of size is resolved by two factors: representativeness (have I collected enough texts (words) to accurately represent the type of language under investigation?) and practicality (time constraints)' (Reppen, 2010: 32). Critical to the consideration of size, therefore, is the aim for the corpus to be 'big enough' to provide a solid representation of the type of language it is intended to represent. The original aim when building CorCenCC was to construct a 10-million-word national corpus that had an equal balance of spoken and written texts (4-million-words each), and 2-million-words of e-language. Given that there were two full-time and one part-time research assistants working on gathering the data over a period of three and a half years, this target was assessed as a potentially achievable aim. In terms of target language, as a 'national' corpus of contemporary Welsh, a decision was made to restrict the collection of language for CorCenCC to the geographical boundary of Wales and not to include the wider Welsh-speaking diaspora (e.g. speakers' resident in the other UK nations) or the Welsh-speaking community in Patagonia. This was to make the collection of data more manageable.

To scaffold data collection using the balanced/sample approach, a design frame was developed. A design frame, also known as a sampling frame, is a rubric that defines which texts, from which genres, and in what proportions are to be sampled for use in a corpus. Design frames also enable users to assess both how suitable a corpus is for undertaking a given line of enquiry and how comparable one corpus is to another. The Brown corpus of American English (Nelson & Kucera, 1967), built in the 1960s, and Lancaster-Oslo-Bergen (LOB) corpus of British English (Johansson et al., 1978), built in the 1970s, are two examples of 'Brown family' corpora that follow the same design frame and are built to be directly comparable. At 1-million-words each, Brown and LOB contain 500 samples of 2000 words across 15 different text categories (akin to genres) including, for example, 'general fiction', 'press: reviews' and 'religion'.

Table 2.1 outlines the initial design frame developed for CorCenCC— as included in the original proposal for the project (and in Knight et al., 2021: 40).

As an initial plan, this design frame sought to incorporate a spread of genres (albeit just 'examples' of these) across the three communicative modes, with a certain amount (and certainly consideration of) balancing, in terms of word count, the different categories. This data was to be sampled from 2015 to 2020 for the spoken and e-language modes and from 2011 to 2020 for the written mode so as to appropriately represent 'contemporary' language use.

26 D. KNIGHT ET AL.

Table 2.1 Original broad design frame for CorCenCC

Mode	Example sources (approximate)	Words	Total
Spoken	Welsh learner discourse	600,000	4 m
	Conversations with friends; with family; televised interviews and TV chat shows (BBC); workplace Welsh	400,000 each	[40%]
	BBC radio shows; service encounters	400,000 each	
	Phone calls; primary, secondary, tertiary, and adult classroom interaction; political speeches; formal and informal interaction at the National Eisteddfod	600,000	
Written	Welsh learner writing	250,000 each	4 m [40%]
	Books; papurau bro (i.e. local community Welsh-language monthlies); political documents; stories	400,000 each	
	Letters and diaries; academic essays; academic textbooks; magazines; adverts, flyers/information leaflets; formal letters	290,000 each	
	Signs	60,000	
E-language	Discussion boards; emails; blogs	500,000 each	2 m [20%]
	Websites, Tweets	300,000	
	Text messages	200,000	

CorCenCC's preliminary design frame was developed when the initial proposal for the project was formulated. It was built from the ground up: informed by the project team's understanding of both the composition of previous corpora, and the Welsh-language context. While this design frame had a useful role when planning the CorCenCC project, it was important to add further evidence-based detail to it when the project commenced. Revised design frames for each mode of data (i.e. spoken, written and e-language) were then developed by the WP1 team before being circulated to the extended project team (that included a range of Welsh-language experts and corpus linguists with extensive experience in building linguistic corpora) for comments/revisions. They were also published in the bi-monthly CorCenCC newsletter, inviting further feedback from the project's wider network of supporters and stakeholders. The statistics/data that informed the targets in these design frames were examined at the start of the CorCenCC project (i.e. 2016), so they relate to this point in time and it is possible that they may have changed since that date.

It is important to underline that a design frame is simply a prototype and that the corpus that is ultimately produced often differs (sometimes quite dramatically) from its initial design. This is because, during the data collection phase, it commonly emerges that certain types/sources of data may not be available as planned, while others not accounted for in the design frame may become available and are appropriate for use. These changes are near impossible to account for in advance. Design frames do, however, offer a useful starting point to building a corpus.

The remainder of this chapter takes each data mode in turn and documents the iterative development and expansion of CorCenCC's initial design frame. By reporting on the specific targets presented, and providing justifications for these, useful guidance for those creating their own corpus design frame(s) emerges. While the points raised in this chapter relate to our experiences of creating design frames for CorCenCC specifically, responses to some useful, generic questions are provided in relation to each data mode. These questions follow:

1. What approach(es) can be used to underpin the development of a corpus design frame?
2. What contexts, types and/or genres of texts can be drawn on when building a corpus?
3. What resources and/or information can be examined as a means of setting data collection targets for corpora?
4. Is there an 'optimal' length that a text should be, to be considered for inclusion in a corpus?
5. In what ways might be it be useful to pilot the development of a corpus?

Similar to all the design frames detailed below is the use of a corpus design taxonomy (i.e. an explicit categorisation scheme) for labelling the properties, types and provenance of texts to be included (more specific genre and context-level taxonomies are discussed below):

- **Mode**: mode of communication (spoken, written, e-language)
- **Context**: socially defined situation of use (e.g. transactional conversations such as buying a cup of tea in a café)
- **Topic**: 'aboutness'/thematic focus of the text (e.g. a factual book about music or a blog about news, media and current affairs)
- **Genre**: distinct rhetorical structure determined by context of culture (e.g. the genre of a magazine, TV programme or a blog)
- **Who**: nature of the relationship between the speakers (e.g. between colleagues or family members)
- **Location**: specific place where the contribution was recorded (e.g. public space)
- **Target audience**: specific age group that a contribution was intended for (e.g. children)
- **Source**: notable contributors to the data—commonly companies/copyright holders (e.g. the Welsh-language TV station S4C)

A range of different taxonomies for classifying corpora exists, depending on, for example, the aims, size and language variety of the corpus. A taxonomy must be consistent and transparent so that corpus users can navigate the corpus with ease. Looking at taxonomies used by other, existing, national corpora can be invaluable in helping to establish your own.

The development of principled design frames for each sub-corpus of CorCenCC's dataset will now be considered in turn, beginning with the spoken sub-corpus.

Spoken Corpora

Spoken corpora are one of the most complex, and often difficult, types of corpora to build (perhaps second only to more multimodal and/or heterogenous corpora, e.g. the Nottingham Multi-Modal Corpus, NMMC, Knight et al., 2006). Unlike its written and digital counterparts, spoken language does not exist in an already computer-readable, text-based format, so requires more time and effort to record/collect, transcribe and process before it can be queried as part of a corpus dataset.

Due to the additional time and labour required in their construction, spoken corpora are often smaller than written corpora. Even where multi-billion-word corpora are concerned, spoken sub-components are typically only a small proportion of the overall dataset, comprising just 10% of the BNC 1994 (Aston & Burnard, 1997) and BNC2014 (Love, Hawtin, et al., 2017) and 4% of the 1.8-billion-word Cambridge English Corpus (CEC, CUP, 2020), for example. Spoken corpora tend to be focused on a specific discourse context and/or community. These include, for example, spoken academic corpora like BASE (British Academic Spoken English, 1.65-million-words, Thompson & Nesi, 2001) and MICASE (Michigan Corpus of Academic Spoken English, 1.7-million-words, Simpson et al., 2000), and spoken business discourse, like CANBEC (Cambridge and Nottingham Business English Corpus, 1-million-words, Handford, 2010). However some, more general, spoken corpora do exist, including HKCSE (Hong Kong Corpus of Spoken English, 200 k words, Cheng & Warren, 1999) and CANCODE (Cambridge and Nottingham Corpus of Discourse in English, 5-million-words, Carter & McCarthy, 2004).

> 1. What approach(es) can be used to underpin the development of a corpus design frame?

McCarthy identifies the following as 'key': the demographic approach and the genre approach (McCarthy, 1998: 8). The demographic approach involves collecting the spoken output of a 'well-chosen population sample' over a given period of time. This approach focuses primarily on the 'who' of language use: capturing language as it is used/produced by a representative sample of a given population.

It has been noted that '[a] corpus constituted solely on the demographic model would [...] omit important spoken text types', such as broadcast interviews, lectures and legal proceedings (Burnard, 2007). This is because, although these types/genres of spoken text are *received* by wide audiences, they are *produced* by few 'speech producers': they are 'produced only rarely in comparison with the total output of all "speech producers"' (Burnard, 2007). While a broad sample of the population *may* be represented in the language collected via the demographic approach, the range of text types used by contributors may, as a result, be quite narrow.

The genre approach aims to mitigate this limitation, seeking to strike a 'balance between speaker, environment, context and recurrent features' (McCarthy, 1998: 8). Using this approach, 'decisions have to made about situational/contextual types as well as population types' (McCarthy, 1998: 9), potentially allowing for a broad range of genres as well as speakers to be represented in a given corpus.

A third approach to building spoken corpora arguably also exists, as used in the development of the Spoken BNC2014: the 'opportunistic' approach (Love, Dembry, et al., 2017: 320). Unlike the previous two approaches, this approach focuses on collecting *any* data that becomes available to the builders of the corpus. With the Spoken BNC2014, the only pre-determined requirement for the data was for it to comprise informal communication. This approach was used because while a range of specialised spoken corpora exists to facilitate the exploration of language use in *specific* contexts, 'there exists greater use of, and demand for, conversational data' in English that is not tied to a specific context (Love, Dembry, et al., 2017: 324). While there is undoubtedly a similar need and use for conversational data in Welsh (i.e. data not tied to a specific context), there is also a need for better representation of language in other, more specific, discursive contexts. Again, as the first 'general' corpus of contemporary Welsh, CorCenCC aimed to provide a resource that represents not only the diversity of Welsh speakers (akin to a more demographic approach, although something that could also be accommodated by the opportunistic approach), but also the wide range of contexts (or spoken genres) in which Welsh is used. To fully enable this, the genre approach, facilitated by a predetermined design frame, was deemed appropriate for use.

2. What contexts, types and/or genres of texts can be drawn on when building a corpus?

A useful starting point to respond to this second question is to examine pre-existing design frames and assess their transferability/reusability to your own discourse context. In the context of CorCenCC, the International Corpus of English (ICE), a set of comparable 1-million-word corpora representing over 20 varieties of English around the world (Kirk & Nelson, 2018), was first examined. Each ICE corpus includes spoken texts categorised into the following genres:

- Dialogues
    - Private: face-to-face conversations, phone calls
    - Public: classroom lessons, broadcast discussions, broadcast interviews, parliamentary debates, legal cross-examinations, business transactions

- Monologues
    - Scripted: broadcast news, broadcast talk, non-broadcast talk
    - Unscripted: spontaneous commentaries, unscripted speeches, demonstrations, legal presentations

Albeit a useful example of a taxonomy of spoken genres, some categories here are assessed as being too broad for use in CorCenCC; others, such as scripted monologues, do not align with CorCenCC's aims of including naturally occurring and/or spontaneous talk. Closer to the aims of CorCenCC is the typology used in CANCODE. CANCODE was built with a particular target audience in mind—language learners— and includes 'unrehearsed, non-formal talk' (McCarthy, 1998: 9), 'in a range of social contexts' (Carter, 1998: 44). Content in CANCODE is balanced, at 20%, across each of the following genres of 'typical goal types' (McCarthy, 1998: 9–10):

- Professional e.g. informal company meetings, staff meetings, desk-to-desk talk
- Pedagogical e.g. informal tutorial conversations, pair, and group-work
- Transactional e.g. day-to-day service encounters in shops, restaurants, etc., between servers and customers, transacting goods, information, or services
- Socialising e.g. a group of friends preparing a party, talking with a stranger on a train
- Intimate e.g. conversations between family members or close friends in private settings

32   D. KNIGHT ET AL.

A different taxonomy/design frame was used for the spoken component of the BNC 1994, which sought to combine data collected via both a demographic and 'context-governed' approach, so as 'to cover the full range of linguistic variation found in spoken language' (Crowdy, 1993: 259). The latter of these is somewhat akin to the genres of typical goal types in CANCODE. However, in the BNC 1994, 'public/institutional' and 'leisure' contexts allowed for the collection of more formal forms of spoken texts not included in CANCODE. The full spoken text typology follows (Crowdy, 1993: 262–264):

- Public/institutional (12.5%) e.g. political speeches, sermons, public/government talks, council meetings, religious meetings, parliamentary proceedings
- Leisure (12.5%) e.g. after dinner speeches, sports commentaries, talks to WI, clubs, etc., broadcast chat shows, phone ins, club meetings
- Business (12.5%) e.g. company talks, trade union speeches, sales demonstrations, business meetings, consultations, interviews
- Educational/Informative (12.5%) e.g. educational demonstrations, lectures and talks, news commentaries, classroom interaction
- Demographic corpus (50%)

As with CANCODE, the BNC 1994's context-governed part includes proportionally equal word counts in each category, resulting in a *balanced* but not necessarily *representative* dataset.

As a starting point in the iterative development of CorCenCC's preliminary design frame (Table 2.1), the taxonomies from CANCODE and the BNC 1994 (as examples of established corpora, albeit in a different source language to CorCenCC) were merged and aligned to produce the following:

- Public/institutional
- Media
- Transactional
- Professional
- Pedagogic
- Socialising
- Private

This taxonomy of seven spoken contexts of language use effectively lies on a cline of formality, from the more institutional and formal (and public-facing)—'public/institutional' and 'media'—to informal and personal contexts—'socialising' and 'private'. Here, context refers to the socially defined situation of use so, for example, buying a cup of tea in a café would be categorised as an interaction carried out in a transactional context. Existing beyond the specific contexts of use are genres, for example sermons and interviews, which are texts/interactions with distinct rhetorical structures (based on Halliday, 1978).

Spoken Contexts

Once the seven spoken contexts were established, a question followed: if the CorCenCC team were to follow the examples set by CANCODE and the BNC 1994, and target the collection of an equal amount of the 4-million-word spoken sub-corpus across these contexts (roughly 571,000 words each), would this offer a 'small scale model' (Atkins et al., 1992: 6) of the Welsh-language community, or would it provide an unjustifiable number of certain genres? Rather than simply balance the data, evidence regarding the nature, and use of language in the spoken Welsh discourse community was sought out as a means for justifying the targets provided in the design frame (accounting for, for example, the numbers, density and distribution of speakers). This evidence-based target setting stage offers a response to the question:

> 3. What resources and/or information can be examined as a means of setting data collection targets for corpora?

A detailed discussion of how CorCenCC's spoken design frame was devised using such evidence will now be presented.

An initial starting point was the Welsh Language Use Survey, a national survey jointly commissioned by the Welsh Language Commissioner and Welsh Government to gain insights into Welsh speakers' fluency, and Welsh-language use across a range of settings. According to the 2013–2015 survey, just over 35% of Welsh speakers use Welsh more than, or just as often as, English at home (National Survey Team, 2015). This equates to over 196,000 people using Welsh at home daily. Guided by these numbers, it seemed justified to aim for a greater proportion of text than the 571,000 represented, and a target of 900,000 words (or 22.5% of the spoken data) to be sourced from 'Private' settings. An even greater number—over 40%, or nearly 225,000 people—use Welsh more, or equally often, than English when talking to friends. Some of these are likely to be in 'private' contexts, and others in 'socialising' contexts, including social, cultural or sporting events or activities. The survey asked 'In the last year, have you attended an organised social or cultural event or activity held in Welsh (e.g. concert, *Eisteddfod*, gig, choir, or society)?' and 'In the last year, have you attended an organised sporting event or activity held in Welsh (e.g. sports club, society or course)?', and those answering 'Yes' represented almost 43% and almost 19% of the Welsh-speaking population, respectively (National Survey Team, 2015). Although the use of Welsh in such contexts may not always occur daily, using Welsh for social purposes is an important discourse domain, so a target word count of 900,000 for the 'socialising' context was set as well.

Welsh-language TV programmes reach audiences of around 173,000 Welsh viewers per week (S4C, 2015: 7), and *Radio Cymru* reaches around 108,000 listeners per week, totalling 281,000 viewers/listeners per week (plus those who listen to Welsh-medium programmes on commercial/community radio stations—Rajar, 2016: 3). Although this is around half the Welsh-speaking population of Wales, this is not a daily activity for all viewers/listeners, so the rounded-up target of 600,000 words (instead of 571,000 words, i.e. 15% of the spoken data) for 'media' is not as high as the targets for 'socialising' and 'private' language.

In response to the Welsh Language Use Survey question 'At work, do you speak Welsh with colleagues?', those who answered 'always' or 'usually' totalled over 32%; and over 25% noted 'always' or 'usually' when asked 'At work, do you speak Welsh with people outside your company/organisation?' (National Survey Team, 2015). Taking an average of 32% and 25% (28.5%) of the Welsh-speaking population equates to just over 160,000 speakers who regularly use Welsh in 'professional' contexts. 'Pedagogic' data also involves participants and audiences of just over 160,000 Welsh speakers (Hughes, 2015). The 'pedagogic' and 'professional' contexts were allocated equal targets (400,000 words each) based on these calculations.

The target for 'transactional' data was also set at 400,000 words, as for day-to-day activities such as shopping or taking the bus, just over 32% of respondents use Welsh as much as, or more than, English; and just over 28% use Welsh 'always' or 'usually' when dealing with public organisations such as the local council (National Survey Team, 2015). Even though these figures were slightly higher than those for 'professional' use of Welsh, it seemed reasonable to assume that more language was produced over the course of a week in workplaces than in transactions. 'Transactional' language was therefore allocated 400,000 words. The remaining 400,000 words was to be the target for 'public/institutional' language. A summary of these targets follows:

- Public/institutional: 400,000 words
- Media: 600,000 words
- Transactional: 400,000 words
- Professional: 400,000 words
- Pedagogic: 400,000 words
- Socialising: 900,000 words
- Private: 900,000 words

The number of conversations/recordings to be sampled from each of these contexts has not been specified here, nor has a minimum or maximum length of recordings been imposed. While it is possible to control the amount of spoken input in corpora of scripted talk, this is not the case where naturally occurring and/or spontaneous talk is to be sourced.

> 4. Is there an 'optimal' length that a text should be, to be considered for inclusion in a corpus?

Typically, the answer is no. It would be difficult to provide an optimum target for this, because naturally occurring talk is highly variable. However, there *is* often a minimum length requirement. For example, the Spoken BNC2014 had no specific targets for data collection across the individual spoken 'strata' of the corpus (due to the opportunistic approach being utilised) but the developers of the corpus 'asked participants to make recordings of no less than 20 minutes in length' (Love, 2020: 45). In major language contexts, it may be advisable to replicate such a minimum requirement, but in more under-resourced/minoritised contexts, this is less appropriate. In these contexts, although it would certainly be quicker and easier to collect fewer texts of longer length, imposing any restrictions is likely to impact on the amount of data that can be sought. To collect as much data as is possible, to reach the targets set by the design frame, more flexibility than this is needed, with shorter (and smaller) texts also being accepted. This potential variability in text length is ultimately likely to lead to more variation in terms of the context of language use and speaker demographics, which is perhaps preferable anyway. The aim for CorCenCC was, however, to include full conversations where possible.

The next step was to devise detailed sub-targets within these categories: determining the broad parameters of the taxonomy (in relation to specific spoken genres and their respective weightings) and defining how and from where the data might be sourced. This step of design frame development is discussed in the following sections.

Public/Institutional

Table 2.2 provides a breakdown of the public/institutional context into specific genres.

The first genre included is 'parliamentary language', based on text-type examples provided by the BNC 1994; with the genre 'political speeches' expanded to include speeches by members of broader political bodies (e.g. Friends of the Earth) as well as public lectures. Deciding how much parliamentary language to target was not a simple task as, although the right to use Welsh in the Welsh Parliament—the *Senedd*—is an important indicator of the status of Welsh, it appears that it is one not exercised by many. For example, in 2015 only 11.8% of contributions in the Chamber of the *Senedd* were made in Welsh (*Cymdeithas yr Iaith Gymraeg* [Welsh Language Society], 2015). A target of 50,000 words was therefore suggested for this category. As political speeches and public lectures, for example, are likely to cover a wide range of subject matters and reach a diverse audience, this genre was allocated substantially more than for parliamentary language, that is 150,000 words.

Table 2.2 Design frame for spoken 'public/institutional' contexts in CorCenCC

Genre	Examples	Words	% spoken sub-corpus	Total
Political speeches and public lectures	e.g. electoral broadcasts, speeches by MPs/AMs/councillors, speeches by the Welsh Language Society, etc., public lectures	150,000	3.75%	400,000 [10%]
Parliamentary language	e.g. parliamentary proceedings	50,000	1.25%	
Formal language at church/chapel	e.g. sermons/homilies, prayers	150,000	3.75%	
Formal language from the National Eisteddfod	e.g. music/dance/recitation/drama adjudications, presentations at university stands/in the Lolfa Lên (Literature Wales)/Maes D (Learners' Tent), etc	50,000	1.25%	

'Formal language at church/chapel' is a specific genre/text type that existed in the BNC 1994, but not in CANCODE nor the Spoken BNC2014. Calculations from a study in 1995 suggested that around 22% of the Welsh-speaking population regularly attend Welsh-language church/chapel services, compared to 8.7% of the population of Wales as a whole (Bible Society, 1997).While these percentages may have decreased since this date, this underlines the importance of this genre in Wales, and provides historical reasons to consider attendance at religious services a noteworthy aspect of Welsh-language culture/life. 150,000 words were allocated to this genre, with an aim to collect sermons/homilies and prayers from a range of Christian denominations, including Anglican, Catholic and Non-conformist (see http://www.cytun.org.uk/us.html for the main denominations in Wales). Hymns were included in CorCenCC's written sub-corpus, and language from less formal aspects of church/chapel life (e.g. youth groups) was categorised as part of the spoken 'socialising' context.

Language from the National *Eisteddfod* is another culturally specific category, as it draws on language from an annual Welsh culture and language festival. The National *Eisteddfod* attracts around 148,000 visitors annually (based on visitor figures from 2008 to 2016, *Eisteddfod Genedlaethol Cymru* [National Eisteddfod of Wales], 2016), but not all of these are Welsh speakers, and it is likely that only a small proportion of visitors are exposed to the language data targeted for collection (i.e. adjudications and talks/presentations). Although the National *Eisteddfod* only runs for one week in every 52, it is an important component of Welsh-language culture. Regarding 'formal language from the National *Eisteddfod*', the aim was to include monologues rather than interaction in this category, so it focussed on talks and presentations given in university tents, *y Lolfa Lên* (the literary tent), *Maes D* (aimed mainly at adult learners of Welsh), etc., as well as adjudications of on-stage competitions. It was decided that the competitions themselves would not be recorded as many involve music, dance or performance of written texts. Adjudications of off-stage competitions are published in writing and are accounted for in the written design frame.

The overall target for spoken *Eisteddfod* data was set at 100,000 words, split 50:50 between formal ('public/institutional') and informal ('socialising') language. The *Urdd Eisteddfod*, aimed at the youth of Wales, is another well-attended Welsh-medium event with some 85,000 visitors over the course of the week (*Urdd Gobaith Cymru*, 2021). Formal spoken language was not to be collected from the *Urdd*, as adjudications here are not presented orally and there are no formal talks/presentations. The genre 'informal interaction at the *Urdd Eisteddfod*' was, however, added to the 'socialising' context, with the aim of collecting data from social spaces such as *Caffi Mistar Urdd* (an on-field café) and the food area.

Table 2.2 does not include any spoken legal language. While participants in legal proceedings in Wales have the right to use Welsh and there is some uptake of this—with over 576 court cases involving Welsh-language use between April 2015 and March 2016—(HM Courts and Tribunals Service Welsh Language Unit, telephone conversation on 08-09-2016), it proved difficult for access to be granted to such data, particularly given that there were plans to make the corpus publicly available. This genre was, therefore, omitted from the revised design frame.

Media

Targets for spoken data from 'media' contexts are detailed in Table 2.3. There are at least 13 commercial or community radio stations

2 DESIGN FRAMES   39

Table 2.3 Design frame for spoken 'media' contexts in CorCenCC

Genre	Genre (specific)	Words	% spoken sub-corpus	Total
TV programmes (BBC/S4C)	Children	135,000	3.375%	330,000 [8.25%]
	Entertainment	51,000	1.275%	
	Factual	50,000	1.25%	
	Drama	36,000	0.9%	
	Sport	36,000	0.9%	
	Music	11,000	0.275%	
	News	11,000	0.275%	
Radio programmes (BBC *Radio Cymru*)	Entertainment	55,000	1.375%	220,000 [5.50%]
	Factual	55,000	1.375%	
	News	44,000	1.1%	
	Music	33,000	0.825%	
	Religion and ethics	11,000	0.275%	
	Sport	11,000	0.275%	
	Comedy	11,000	0.275%	
Commercial/community radio		50,000	1.25%	50,000 [1.25%]
		600,000	15%	

committed to the use and/or promotion of Welsh (Ofcom, 2015), as well as BBC/S4C television (TV) and radio broadcasts. The targets for BBC/S4C programmes were divided 60:40 between TV and radio. The justification for this was their viewing/listening figures, with circa 173,000 viewers of S4C (S4C, 2015: 7) and 108,000 people listening to *Radio Cymru* per week (Rajar, 2016: 3). The total number of viewers/listeners was 281,000 per week, with circa 60% watching S4C and 40% listening to *Radio Cymru*. The remainder is dedicated to commercial/community radio where Welsh-language programmes are often one element in the wider provision. The target for this genre is significantly smaller than for *Radio Cymru* radio programmes because these channels do not provide programming that is exclusively in Welsh, and it is therefore unlikely that a large amount of Welsh-language data would be available.

The genres for *Radio Cymru* programmes listed are based on the number of hours each category is broadcast over a typical week. For example, in the week beginning Monday 25th April 2016, almost 25 hours each of 'entertainment' and 'factual' radio programmes were scheduled, around 20 hours of 'news' programmes (although these are likely to be repetitive over the course of a given day) and up to five hours each of the 'religion and ethics', 'sport' and 'comedy' programmes. The TV programme timetable (S4C, 2016) for 27 April to 3 May 2016 included over 45 hours of children's programmes. The next largest categories were 'entertainment' and 'factual', then 'sports', 'music' and 'drama'. The targets for each were set accordingly, although fewer words were targeted at 'music' programmes as lyrics from music itself were not to be included. News programmes were broadcast for only 4.25 hours per week, hence the small target for this genre.

Transactional

As CorCenCC's design frame focuses on external rather than internal properties of texts (i.e. the properties of the language contained within the text itself), genres in the 'transactional' category (Table 2.4) are classified based on the context in which the interaction takes place, rather than the specifics of the conversation within it. It was proposed to sample from a range of sectors, inspired by *Lleol.Cymru's* directory of Welsh-speaking service providers and Welsh-language helplines (Lleol.net, 2014), to represent services available through the medium of Welsh.

A comprehensive list of dedicated Welsh-language phone lines is provided at http://www.cymorth.com/. The list on this website categorises service providers according to the following: education, financial, utilities, media, charities and government. Over 50% of service providers fall under the 'government' category. Although it is not possible to quantify the exact uptake of these services, the number of providers in each category provides an indication of demand for them, so it seemed appropriate to aim to collect substantially more service transaction data from government and public sector settings than others. The remaining genres merged the phone line categories with those from the *Lleol.Cymru* directory, with data collection targets based roughly on the number of services available, and on the practicalities of collecting the data. 'Education' was omitted given the education-related data already included in the 'pedagogic' context. Only a small proportion of the data was allocated to financial, legal and health settings, given the potential difficulties of recording conversations involving sensitive information.

2 DESIGN FRAMES 41

Table 2.4 Design frame for spoken 'transactional' contexts in CorCenCC

Genre	Genre (specific)	Words	% spoken sub-corpus	Total
Transacting goods, information, and services (face-to-face or phone calls)	Public sector, e.g. councils, Welsh Language Commissioner's office, post offices, HMRC, libraries	140,000	3.5%	400,000 [10%]
	Retail, e.g. shops, auctions	60,000	1.5%	
	Food, e.g. restaurants, cafes	60,000	1.5%	
	Tourism and travel, e.g. tourist information, accommodation, national rail enquiries	60,000	1.5%	
	Leisure, e.g. media, clubs, entertainment, beauty	60,000	1.5%	
	Finance, law, and health, e.g. accountants, solicitors, clinics, pharmacies, hospitals	20,000	0.5%	

Professional

The 'professional' context (Table 2.5) includes business-to-business and internal phone calls (with customer-to-business phone calls categorised as 'service encounters'). Phone calls include any conversations carried out using telephones, mobile phones, Skype, WhatsApp, Facetime, etc. The genres 'staff meetings', 'interviews' and 'desk-to-desk conversation' were also added based on the taxonomies provided by CANCODE and the BNC 1994. Meetings and interviews included those carried out virtually, as well as face-to-face. It was particularly difficult to propose principled targets for these specific categories as it is near to impossible to predict, for example, how often phone calls would be made and how much data was likely to be accessible/available.

42   D. KNIGHT ET AL.

Table 2.5   Design frame for spoken 'professional' contexts in CorCenCC

Genre	Genre (specific)	Words	% spoken sub-corpus	Total
Workplace Welsh	Meetings	100,000	2.5%	400,000
	Interviews	100,000	2.5%	[10%]
	Desk-to-desk conversation	100,000	2.5%	
	Business-to-business interaction (face-to-face or phone calls)	50,000	1.25%	
	Internal phone calls	50,000	1.25%	

Pedagogic

Data in the 'pedagogic' context focuses on teacher-student(s) and student–student(s) interaction, with proportions of each varying depending on subject, teaching style and level. The aim was to sample language from Welsh-medium, English-medium and bilingual institutions, at all levels of education (primary, secondary, tertiary and adult), and all lesson types (classes, lectures, tutorials, seminars, workshops, practicals). This is seen in Table 2.6.

A schools' census conducted in 2015 showed that there were 65,460 pupils in Welsh-medium/bilingual primary schools (Hughes, 2015: 5). This number is larger than the number of pupils in any other Welsh-medium/bilingual education type, so was allocated the largest portion (35%) of the data in this context. The schools' census (Hughes, 2015: 5) also showed that there were 38,933 pupils in Welsh-medium/bilingual secondary/middle schools and they were allocated 25% of the data in this context. The proportions of Welsh and English used are likely to vary between schools, so only data from lessons taught through the medium of Welsh was collected.

The largest subject areas (other than Welsh itself) taught through Welsh at secondary school level were sciences/maths (>12,000 exam candidates per year), art/drama/music (>3000 candidates per year) and geography/history/religious studies (circa 7000 candidates per year), based on the average number of GCSE, AS- and A-Level candidates who chose to sit their exams through the medium of Welsh in 2010 and 2015 (WJEC, 2015). Regarding Welsh as a subject, 19,245 pupils were working towards exams in Welsh language and literature through the medium of

2 DESIGN FRAMES 43

Table 2.6 Design frame for spoken 'pedagogic' contexts in CorCenCC

Genre	Topics	Words	% spoken sub-corpus	Total
Primary classroom interaction	Welsh-medium classroom interaction (various ages)	140,000	3.5%	140,000 [3.5%]
Secondary classroom interaction	Welsh-medium science and maths lessons	40,000	1%	120,000 [3%]
	Welsh-medium art, drama, and music lessons	15,000	0.375%	
	Welsh-medium geography, history, and religious studies lessons	30,000	0.75%	
	Welsh-medium Welsh lessons	35,000	0.875%	
Secondary and FE classroom interaction	Welsh (second language) lessons in English-medium schools/colleges	30,000	0.75%	30,000 [0.75%]
FE classroom interaction	Welsh-medium lessons in a variety of subjects, e.g. Basic skills, Cultural studies, Health care, IT	40,000	1%	40,000 [1%]
HE classroom interaction	Welsh-medium HE lessons in a variety of subjects, e.g. Linguistics, Arts, Medicine	20,000	0.5%	20,000 [0.5%]
Adult classroom interaction	Welsh-medium community education	20,000	0.5%	20,000 [0.5%]
	Adult Welsh lessons	30,000	0.75%	30,000 [0.75%]
		400,000	10%	

Welsh in 2011 (WJEC, 2012). This informed the relatively large target for Welsh-medium Welsh lessons.

Data was also to be collected from Welsh lessons in English-medium secondary schools. In 2011, around 21,108 pupils were working towards non-compulsory GCSE, AS- and A-Level Welsh in English-medium schools (WJEC, 2012). There were also around 26,475 years 10/11 pupils studying compulsory GCSE Welsh in English-medium schools (based on exam candidates in 2011/2012, WJEC, 2012) and thousands more studying the subject in years 7–9. Despite the high numbers, it seemed appropriate to collect substantially less data from these Welsh lessons, since pupils at English-medium schools have only a few hours' Welsh tuition per week. In addition, Welsh is only compulsory up to the age of 16, so there are many pupils who receive no Welsh tuition at all post-GCSE.

At primary school level, there is not such a clear division between subject areas so there was an agreed aim to include a variety of age groups rather than specific subjects (in Welsh-medium schools). Data would not be collected from Welsh lessons in English-medium primary schools, as similar data was already represented at secondary school level.

Tertiary education includes FE (Further Education) and HE (Higher Education), and data was to be collected from Welsh-medium lessons at both levels. For HE, the most popular Welsh-medium subject areas are communication/linguistics/literature, arts/humanities and medicine/science (*Coleg Cymraeg Cenedlaethol* [National Welsh College], 2014): data would include interaction from a variety of subject areas. In FE, the most popular subjects studied through the medium of Welsh or bilingually were 'care/personal development', 'cultural studies/languages/literature', 'health care/medicine/health and safety' and 'information technology and information' (Welsh Government, 2015). At FE level, it is also possible to study Welsh through the medium of English. Some classroom interaction from English-medium Welsh lessons would come from FE institutions. Data collection can be maximised by targeting several classes in the same day/couple of days as well as those that are likely to involve more discussion and spoken activities.

Socialising and Private

Genres in the 'socialising' and 'private' contexts are inspired by categories from CANCODE and were expanded according to how location and interlocutor relationships might affect a speaker's language use. These are depicted in Tables 2.7 and 2.8, respectively.

Certain categories in CANCODE, such as 'a group of friends preparing a party' have not been included, given that they are too specific, and task focused (CorCenCC aimed to be more general than this). There is a

2 DESIGN FRAMES   45

Table 2.7 Design frame for spoken 'socialising' contexts in CorCenCC

Genre	Locations	Words	% spoken sub-corpus	Total
Conversations with friends/family	In the home (e.g. party, dinner, barbecue)	280,000	7%	820,000 [20.5%]
	In public places (e.g. pubs, restaurants)	270,000	6.75%	
	During leisure activities (e.g. clubs, societies, churches)	270,000	6.75%	
Informal interaction at the National Eisteddfod	Conversations in social spaces such as the Merched y Wawr tent, Maes D	50,000	1.25%	50,000 [1.25%]
Informal interaction at the Urdd Eisteddfod	Conversations in social spaces such as the food area, Caffi Mistar Urdd	30,000	0.75%	30,000 [0.75%]
		900,000	22.5%	

Table 2.8 Design frame for spoken 'private' contexts in CorCenCC

Genre	Genres (specific)	Words	% spoken sub-corpus	Total
Conversations with family	Parent(s)-child(ren) conversations	170,000	4.25%	580,000 [14.5%]
	Conversations with spouses and partners	170,000	4.25%	
	Conversations between other family members	160,000	4%	
	Phone calls to family members	80,000	2%	
Conversations with friends	Conversations with housemates	120,000	3%	320,000 [8%]
	Conversations with close friends in private settings	120,000	3%	
	Phone calls to close friends	80,000	2%	
		900,000	22.5%	

certain amount of overlap/similarity between the genres of socialising and private contexts and for this reason both contexts are considered here. While there are many locations in which one can socialise, the genres of 'socialising' are discrete, whereas the 'private' context crosses many different genres rather than being tied to specific, definable locations. Therefore, the design frames for each of these focus on locations for the former and genres for the latter. A target of 900,000 was assigned to each of these contexts—these are likely to be where speakers most frequently use Welsh, so they represent the highest proportions of the corpus.

In the next chapter, there is a brief discussion of some of the demographic-related targets for the spoken sub-corpus and Chapter 5 examines to what extent plans were realised. Details of how to create design frames for written language will now be presented, again drawing on the experiences of building CorCenCC.

WRITTEN CORPORA

Early digitised national corpora contained predominantly written texts. Brown and LOB are notable examples of such corpora (discussed above), as are the 4.5-million-word Bank of English, which was built in the 1980s (this now forms part of the 550-million-word COBUILD corpus, Sinclair, 1987), and the 100-million-word BNC 1994 (90% of which was written, Aston & Burnard, 1997). With the onset of the digital age, the size, scale and availability of written corpora have grown exponentially.

Broadly speaking, there are seven types of written corpora (adapted from Gardner & Moreton, 2020: 28):

1. General: intended to reflect general uses of spoken and written language
2. Historical/diachronic: texts from specific periods, or allowing comparison by, e.g. decade
3. Learner: texts produced by learners
4. Monitor: corpora that are regularly updated to track changes in a language
5. Parallel: texts and their aligned translation(s)
6. Multilingual: texts in several languages
7. Specialist: designed for a specific purpose with specific types of texts (e.g. academic discourse)

'Texts' in a written corpus are 'often assumed to be a series of coherent sentences and paragraphs' (Atkins et al., 1992: 2). Texts can be public or private facing, widely published or not published, produced by one or numerous contributors and so on. The broad design/type of a written corpus (or sub-corpus) helps to determine the specific type of texts to include.

A consideration of *text type* in corpus design focuses on the internal criteria/properties of specific texts, while *genre* focuses on the external criteria of a text. As noted above, a genre is a text's distinct rhetorical structure determined by context of culture (e.g. the genre of a magazine, TV programme or a blog). A consideration of genre is often seen as more appropriate than text type when building corpora (Biber, 1994; McEnery et al., 2006), as it 'is the level of categorisation which is theoretically and pedagogically the most useful and most practical to work with' (Lee, 2001: 37). This informed the design of CorCenCC's written sub-corpus, readdressing the question:

> 1. What approach(es) can be used to underpin the development of a corpus design frame?

Building written (and e-language) corpora is generally more straightforward than spoken corpora as written language 'data' typically exists in a text-based format from the start. Despite this, a close consideration of the genres to be included, how many are needed, how much of each text and genre to include (and from what points in the text(s)), how the number and samples of texts are balanced (if at all) across the genres, and whether you are able, and have the right, to access and (re)use the data in the way you desire to use it, is required.

Size and Sampling

The original target size for CorCenCC's written sub-corpus was 4-million-words (Table 2.1), to be sampled from texts of different lengths, from a range of Welsh-language genres, that are targeted at different readers.

> **4. Is there an 'optimal' length that a text should be, to be considered for inclusion in a corpus?**

There is extensive discussion on whether or not one should strive to include whole texts or chunks of texts in written corpora (and in what quantities), as well as which sections/chunks should be included (Hunston, 2008; McEnery et al., 2006; Sinclair, 1991). While including full texts would arguably be preferable (as was seen with spoken corpora above), issues relating to copyright and access can impact on the extent to which this is possible. A 'prototypical' target of 5000 words was used when building the Written BNC2014, for example, although 'for some genres of texts which were particularly difficult to collect, this sample size was increased to allow more text to be collected from fewer sources' (Hawtin, 2018: 116). The maximum sample size used in the Thai National Corpus (TNC) was 40,000 words, with up to 90% of texts being used (Aroonmanakun et al., 2009). Sample size needs careful consideration at a local level.

The number of new texts published every year in Welsh is relatively small compared to major language contexts. In 2018–2019, for example, 231 Welsh-language books and 15 Welsh-language magazines were published, meaning there is potentially only a small number of texts to sample from (even without considering challenges relating to accessing/reusing the texts). Consequently, relatively large samples were required from each text to help meet the 4-million-word target in CorCenCC. The default sample size for most texts was set at 10,000 words (with all of text used if it was less than 10,000 words in total). Up to 30% of published books was sampled typically from three points: chapter/section two (to avoid formulaic conventions in opening and closing chapters), central section(s) or chapter(s) and the penultimate section or chapter. Although the length of books for adults varies considerably, it was reasonable to predict an average of 50,000 words per volume, on which basis circa 15,000 words from each were sampled. Regarding dictionaries and grammar books, the introduction/introductory chapter(s) were sampled along with descriptive/explanatory passages in the body of the text. Lists of words (as in the main body of a dictionary) were omitted.

2. What contexts, types and/or genres of texts can be drawn on when building a corpus?
3. What resources and/or information can be examined as a means of setting data collection targets for corpora?

The following sections offer further case-study-based responses to the second and third questions by exploring the different types and/or genres of texts that can be drawn on when developing a written design frame for the Welsh-language context, as well as the resources and/or information that can be examined as a means for setting targets in such a design frame.

Sampling and Categorising Written Welsh

To create CorCenCC's written design frame, a closer consideration was given to both the number of texts written in Welsh (authorship) and the number of Welsh-language texts that are purchased and/or read (readership). In the design frames presented in Tables 2.9–2.11, an attempt has been made to achieve a certain level of balance across genre and word count, but also to represent publishing industry activity and the availability of volumes currently in print, so targets would be both principled and achievable. Written texts were to include those in print within the period of 2015–2020, with the publication date noted in the metadata, along with information on whether the volume was a reprint, and if so, the publication date of the first edition.

The first genre considered was Welsh-language books. Wales has an active Welsh-language publishing industry, with 3698 Welsh-language books for adults and 5565 Welsh-language books for children in print in 2012 (Gwales.com, 2012). Particularly noteworthy is that, 'the children's book industry in Wales is currently enjoying a sustained period of growth and vitality unparalleled in any other area of the Welsh book industry' (Rosser, 2012: 1). This reflects the resurgence in the number of young people who can speak the language, due largely to the availability of Welsh-medium education. With almost 38% of all Welsh speakers being represented in the 3–19 years age category (ONS, 2011), it was important to represent books for children in the corpus. This particular type of text has added significance when considering the readership of such

Table 2.9 Design frame for books in CorCenCC

Target readers	Genre	Topic	Words	% written sub-corpus	Total
Books for adults	Fiction	Drama	50,000	1.25%	880,000 [22%]
		Poetry	100,000	2.5%	
		Prose	250,000	6.25%	
	Eisteddfod (National): compositions/adjudications		50,000	1.25%	
	Factual	Humanities, arts	20,000	0.5%	
		Natural science, medicine, social science	20,000	0.5%	
		Law, politics, education	10,000	0.25%	
		Economics, business, maths, accountancy	10,000	0.25%	
		Travel, tourism	10,000	0.25%	
		Leisure, cookery, puzzles	40,000	1%	
		Wales, local history, local customs	40,000	1%	
		Biographies, autobiographies	240,000	6%	
	Grammar/language/dictionaries		20,000	0.5%	
	Songs/hymns		20,000	0.5%	
Books for children	Fiction	Drama	50,000	1.25%	450,000 [11.25%]
		Poetry	50,000	1.25%	
		Prose: secondary	70,000		

Target readers	Genre	Topic	Words	% written sub-corpus	Total
		Prose: primary & nursery	50,000	1.75%	
				1.25%	
	Eisteddfod (Urdd) compositions, etc		50,000	1.25%	
	Factual	Course books	50,000	1.25%	
		Factual: secondary	50,000	1.25%	
		Factual: primary & nursery	50,000	1.25%	
	Grammar/language/dictionaries		10,000	0.25%	
	Songs, nursery rhymes, hymns		20,000	0.5%	
Books for adult learners	Fiction		50,000	1.25%	160,000 [4%]
	Factual		50,000	1.25%	
	Factual: course books		50,000	1.25%	
	Grammar/language/dictionaries		10,000	0.25%	
Books for young learners	Fiction: secondary		30,000	0.75%	140,000 [3.5%]
	Fiction: primary and nursery		10,000	0.25%	
	Factual: Course books		30,000	0.75%	
	Factual: secondary		30,000	0.75%	
	Factual: primary and nursery		30,000	0.75%	
	Grammar/language/dictionaries		10,000	0.25%	
			1,630,000	40.75%	

books, as they are read by a high proportion of adults as well as children (to assist children).

Regarding the readership of Welsh-language books, no one single source provides adequate information on which to base a design frame. Sales figures are not necessarily a reliable indicator of readership. The number of books currently in print does, however, give some indication of readership above and beyond actual publication figures, so was deemed a useful resource to draw on. The Welsh Books Council, a Welsh Government funded body that exists to promote the publishing industry in Wales, has a comprehensive website (www.gwales.com) that includes an online catalogue of Welsh-language books, journals and magazines currently in print. This site provided useful input for defining the genres in Table 2.9. Ideally, the sample of books for adults would contain a cross-section of the major genres e.g. Fantasy, Science Fiction, Romance, Historical Fiction, Humour, Detective or Spy, Utopia or Dystopia, Urban Fiction, Rural Fiction, Post-modernism/Magical Realism, Political/Satirical Fiction, Feminist Fiction, Queer Fiction/Fiction with LGBT themes, where possible, although these specific sub-categories are not included in this design frame.

The results of the Welsh Books Council's study of book buying and reading habits were also drawn on here (Welsh Books Council, 2012). This study, which focused on 1000 respondents, indicated that the types and genres of books read differed according to location, gender, age and socio-economic group. The 'general' readership of different Welsh-language books was indicated to be as follows (noting the percentage of the sample who read each 'type' of book): 53% novels/fiction; 45% books for children; 41% biographies/memoirs; 39% factual books; 28% poetry; 14% books for learners and 4% other. These categories, and the statistical distribution of readership, informed the final design frame for 'books' in the written sub-corpus in Table 2.9. 'Books' are sub-categorised according to their target readers/audience, and capture written data for adult learners, and child learners as well as just for adults and children.

Given:

i. the scant number of academic volumes and technical and vocational publications that are published in Welsh annually (mainly by the University of Wales Press i.e. 0 in 2015 and 9 in 2014, for example—Gwales.com, 2012), and that

ii. it is common for publishing houses/presses to publish books that straddle the academic and non-academic spheres (e.g. *Y Lolfa* publish books in the series *Astudiaethau Athronyddol* [Philosophical Studies]),

it was decided not to make a distinction between academic and non-academic books but rather categorise them according to subject matter.

The results of the Welsh Books Council study (2012) also indicated that, for example, women are more likely to read fiction and men to read factual books, and those from the highest socio-economic group were more likely to read poetry. These findings were considered when composing the written design, but there was a decision made against setting specific demographic targets such as age, fluency and geography as this was deemed too restrictive and might impact on what could be collected. What was accounted for, however, is the fact that a lower number of individuals can read and write in Welsh compared to those who can speak it (2011 census, ONS, 2011). This suggests that the sources of written Welsh available are likely to be more formal than in spoken contexts, and from a smaller number and demographic spread of contributors.

The initial design frame in Table 2.1 neglected to include texts from National *Eisteddfod* Compositions and Adjudications. These have subsequently been added into the revised frame as they have important cultural status in the Welsh-language context. Table 2.1 also proposes collecting 600,000 words of learner writing (with genres more explicitly defined than in the initial design frame), while only 400,000 words of books. When revisiting these figures, they seemed vastly disproportionate, especially in the light of publication and readership figures available from the Welsh Books Council. Just over 500 titles for adult and child Welsh learners are listed on the www.gwales.com website as compared to over 9000 titles for child and adult expert speakers. It is also unclear whether Welsh learner writing referred to text produced by Welsh learners or text produced for use by Welsh learners. These word counts were therefore revised to make them more proportionate and representative of the genres.

Table 2.10 provides the design frame for the magazines, newspapers and journals in CorCenCC (sampled from the same period as books). There is a predominance of words proposed for '*papurau bro*', local community Welsh-language monthlies that have multiple authorship

Table 2.10 Design frame for magazines, newspapers and journals in CorCenCC

Genre	Topic	Target audience	Words	% written sub-corpus	Total
Papurau bro			400,000	10%	770,000
Journals	Academic, arts, music, literature		70,000	1.75%	[19.25%]
Society magazines/ newsletters	Arts, music, literature Nature Science Agriculture Women Religion		70,000	1.75%	
Newspapers: monthly			50,000	1.25%	
Periodicals: weekly			50,000	1.25%	
Periodicals: monthly			50,000	1.25%	
Magazines		Children: secondary	20,000	0.5%	
		Children: primary	20,000	0.5%	
		Learners: adults	20,000	0.5%	
		Learners: children	20,000	0.5%	

(https://papuraubro.cymru/). There are some 60 *papurau bro* covering most areas of Wales, so there was an effort to ensure that they were sampled from a variety of geographical communities, as each has its own particular emphasis, areas of expertise and regional flavour.

There was an aim to collect 70,000 words from 'academic journals' specifically as there is comparatively little in the broader academic domain in Welsh and these sources provide examples of written Welsh of a formal variety.

Many local societies who operate through the medium of Welsh produce magazines and periodicals, so this category was also incorporated into the design frame. This is accompanied by more general Welsh-language magazines, targeted at speakers of different ages and levels of ability (although the readership of such texts is likely to be low). There are no daily newspapers in the Welsh language so while these may be included in written corpora in other languages, this was not possible here.

Table 2.11 Design frame for miscellaneous written data in CorCenCC

Genre	Words	% written sub-corpus	Total
Letters and diaries	200,000	5%	1,600,000
		5%	[40%]
Formal letters	200,000		
Academic essays, exam scripts	200,000	5%	
Advertisements	100,000	2.5%	
Information leaflets, political documents, legal documents	250,000	6.25%	
Stories	400,000	10%	
Signs	60,000	1.5%	
Other	190,000	4.75%	

Table 2.11 accounts for the 'miscellaneous' documents to be collected. These include a range of formally produced and public-facing documents ('information leaflets, political documents, legal documents', 'signs' and 'advertisements'), to more informal texts ('personal letters and diaries').

The genres included here are important as they likely represent the types of texts that are encountered/received on a regular basis by Welsh-language speakers (i.e. in their daily lives). The texts in this miscellaneous category aim to represent a range of dialects and registers, and most are written to be accessible to all levels of language expertise.

In addition to published material, there was a plan to collect written materials from a diverse range of individuals and companies/institutions, etc., to reflect the variety of ways in which the Welsh language is currently used.

Having defined the design frames for the spoken and written sub-corpora, attention can now be turned to the third mode of data included in CorCenCC: e-language.

DEFINING E-LANGUAGE

Digital communication is ubiquitous in the modern world and has an impact on how people work, socialise, communicate and, ultimately, live. Gaining a better understanding of the ways in which discourse is used to scaffold existence in this digital world has emerged as a priority area for applied linguistics research. Corpus linguists are ideally situated to contribute to this work as they have the appropriate expertise to construct, analyse and characterise patterns of language use in large-scale bodies of digital discourse.

In the planning and building of CorCenCC any digitally based communicative, interactive and/or linguistic stimulus that 'incorporates multiple forms of media bridging the physical and digital' (Heer & Boyd, 2005: 1) was considered to be a form of 'e-language'. E-language exists in a text-based form (albeit digital), so its *physical representation* is somewhat akin to 'written' language. However, while written forms of communication are traditionally asynchronous, meaning that there is often a delay between the point at which a text is written and read/received by its audience, this is not the case for e-language. The use of digital technology in e-language communication instead affords a 'reduction of the temporal and social distance between the sender and receiver' (Knight, 2015: 20), equating to it being more immediate, and synchronous. The properties of *transmission* and *receipt* of e-language are therefore more aligned to a spoken than written form of communication (for discussions of (a)synchronicity in different communicative modes, see Condon & Cech, 1996; Herring, 2007; Knight, 2015; Ko, 1996). This notion of synchronicity blurs the boundaries of traditional conceptions of 'written' and 'spoken' communication in 'e-language'.

A detailed investigation of the similarities and differences in language use across different communicative modes, and this idea of 'blurring', is something that, to date, has been underexplored in many minoritised language contexts, including Welsh. Enabling users to undertake this area of enquiry is something that can be achieved using an e-language (sub)corpus.

Genres of e-Language

> 2. What contexts, types and/or genres of texts can be drawn on when building a corpus?

Revisiting this question, some key genres of e-language include: blogs, websites, discussion boards, social networking updates (e.g. Tweets), emails and SMS messages. First, blogs, which share similar layouts and/or formats to websites, often comprise numerous text-based posts (or images), hyperlinked lists/archives of recent posts and keywords, an area where readers can provide comments and so on. Like an online diary or journal, blogs are typically associated with a single 'blogger', who contributes/posts to a website/page that focuses on specific topics and/or themes. Blogs often include extended pieces of prose as they are not restricted by space or word count. There are also no restrictions on who can write/publish a blog. Blogs are thought to account for 30% of the entire web, primarily comprising texts of 6 main topics/genres: news, sport, opinion, personal narrative, informational and travel (Biber et al., 2015).

Non-blogging 'websites', in comparison, are typically more formal and static in content, with multiple authors involved in their design and presentation. They are also often more general and/or publicly targeted in their readership. It was in acknowledgement of these key differences in structure, composition and readership that blogs were treated as a distinct form of website in the design of CorCenCC.

Discussion boards, sometimes known as 'discussion forums', 'message boards' and 'online forums', are an internet resource that enables users to 'post messages that can then be read and responded to by others' (Yiğit, 2005: 3). Discussion boards provide space for interaction between multiple users and, again, focus on specific themes/topics/areas of interest.

Social networking sites (SNSs) enable users to post short comments (280 characters in the case of individual Tweets) about their thoughts, feelings, reflections, etc. to specific followers, friends and/or the world at large. Examples of SNSs include Twitter (www.twitter.com), Facebook (www.facebook.com), Instagram (www.instagram.com), among others. SNSs can be used on a personal level or professionally, for publicity and advertising. Tweets are typically outward facing, so can be accessed, and read by anyone, although this is not necessarily the case for other SNSs.

Emails, in contrast to Tweets, are a more private, and often formal, form of digital communication than those previously discussed. Other than, for example, emails sent to multiple (typically known) recipients by a company to market goods, emails sent to newsletter subscribers, or jokes forwarded to friends and colleagues, email content is generally not widely shared.

SMSs (short message service), also known as text or instant messages (IMs), are also traditionally more private forms of digital communication that are sent between a known receiver and one or many recipients. An SMS is typically restricted in word count and shorter in length than other forms of e-language, aside from some SNS contributions. Interestingly, this form of messaging 'was never originally envisioned as a means of communication between individuals ... it was originally conceived of as having commercial use, or possibly as a service for mobile phones to signal the arrival of a voicemail message' (Crystal, 2008: 77), but its use in modern life is ubiquitous. In recent years there has been a wealth of new digital applications that offer users the option of sending short, immediate, text-based messages, such as WhatsApp (www.wha tsapp.com), Facebook Messenger (www.messenger.com), among others. When building CorCenCC, the label 'SMS messages' was used to relate to any short electronic text message sent from any text-based messaging services (i.e. encompassing all these forms of short, immediate, text-based messages).

E-Language Corpora

A range of e-language corpora already exists and provides useful models for further corpus building. Mark Davies' corpus portal www.english-corpora.org, for example, provides extensive and widely used web-based corpora, including the 1.9-billion-word Wikipedia, 1.9-billion-word Global Web-Based English (GloWbE, Davies & Fuchs, 2015) and 8.7-billion-word News on the Web (NOW, Davies, 2016) corpora. A particularly innovative corpus on this site is iWeb (Intelligent Web-based Corpus) which extends to over 14-billion-words of English. iWeb, which was designed for teaching, learning and research, includes data from 22-million web pages/sites harvested in a 'systematic way', with samples of 240 web pages and around 145,000 words from each. This design enables users to create their own small 'virtual corpora' that draw on specific topics/pages in this dataset, and to undertake word and phrase searches and generate frequency lists.

Other notable e-language corpora include UKWaC (UK Web as a Corpus, Ferraresi et al., 2008), with over 2-million-tokens of English, and the 10-billion-word EnTenTen web-crawled corpus of English (this also includes 10-billion-words for over 35 other languages, making it a comparable corpus, Jakubíček et al., 2013). Both of these corpora are available through Sketch Engine (Kilgarriff et al., 2010). Other e-language corpora include the 140-million-word Blog Authorship Corpus (Schler et al., 2006), CorText corpus of 110,000 words from SMS messages (Tagg, 2009), ENRON email corpus (71-million-word email corpus, Klimt & Yang, 2004), NPS Chat Corpus (10,567 messages from online chat rooms, Forsyth & Martell, 2007) and the Welsh e-language corpora mentioned in Chapter 1 (also see Knight et al., 2021: 25–27 for a more detailed overview of current Welsh language corpora).

> 1. What approach(es) can be used to underpin the development of a corpus design frame?

There are essentially two main types of e-based corpora: those that are 'designed' and those that are 'crawled' (Kilgarriff et al., 2010). Much like the difference between the sample/genre-based and opportunistic approaches discussed in reference to the spoken and written sub-corpora above, 'the content of a designed [e-language] corpus is selected based on its design specification whereas there is much less control on the content of a corpus constructed by crawling the web' (Asheghi et al., 2014: 1341). Most of the e-language corpora mentioned thus far were collected via web-crawling techniques (i.e. using a computer programme, a 'crawler', that is employed to search, download and automatically index content from the web). They are also typically specialist in nature, insofar as they usually contain one specific genre of e-language (i.e. website, SMS etc.), even in cases where the datasets extend to billions of words.

Until recently, general, 'national' corpora have not included e-language data, making its addition in CorCenCC both timely and invaluable. Exceptions to this include the CRFC (Corpus de référence du français contemporain, Siepmann et al., 2015) and the Written BNC2014 (Hawtin, 2018). In the latter of these corpora, e-language is included as part of the 'written' mode (rather than as a distinct e-language sub-corpus), comprising 11% of the 100-million-word dataset, with data from blogs, microblogs (Tweets), discussion forums, emails, instant messages, reviews and comments.

One of the only corpora that includes a range of different genres of e-language, and utilised a principled design frame in its development, is CANELC (Cambridge and Nottingham e-Language Corpus, Knight et al., 2014), a 1-million-word corpus including Tweets, blogs, discussion boards, SMSs and emails. CANELC was used to inform the development of the Written BNC2014 and is now included in the wider Cambridge English Corpus (CUP, 2020) which is privately owned and not publicly accessible.

CANELC initially aimed to include contributions from a range of sociolinguistically profiled participants, with word counts to be balanced across genres. The final composition of the corpus included a fairly consistent number of words sourced from blogs, discussion board content and Tweets (i.e. circa 25%, 250,000 words each), with the number of words from SMSs and emails, combined, constituting the final 25%. Given their restricted character length, the number of individual messages/entries from Tweets is considerably higher than the other forms of e-language data.

SMSs and emails were not categorised in CANELC, while the blogs, discussion boards and Tweets were thematically classified, as follows:

A. News, media and current affairs; politics; business and finance; weather and the environment
B. Culture, literature and the arts; fashion; teaching, academia and education
C. Technology, computer and gaming; hobbies and pastimes; travel; cookery
D. Music; sport
E. Celebrity news and gossip; TV; humour
F. Health and beauty; parenting and family life; personal and daily life

These themes and topics exist on a continuum from more 'public' concerns (category 'A') such as news, politics, and current affairs, to the 'private' (e.g. personal and daily life—category 'F').

When considering how to classify e-language topics for CorCenCC, a pre-existing categorisation scheme that could be adapted/modified both because of the findings from an e-language pilot (see below) and as a result of issues and challenges faced as the collection phase progressed was sought. Given Knight's familiarity with the CANELC coding scheme, and the fact that it was partially used in the Written BNC2014, this scheme was deemed to be a suitable guiding principle here.

CANELC's scheme is just one approach to classifying e-language, however. As with much of the categorisation and labelling of texts in corpora, 'there is no agreed set of genre labels so that each collections' labels vary according to researchers' priorities and the genre definition chosen' (Asheghi et al., 2016: 607). Alternative taxonomies (predominantly for website classification) exist including Biber et al., (2015), Stubbe et al., (2007), Biber et al., (2015), Asheghi et al., (2016) and Biber and Egbert (2018).

Piloting Corpus Building

While e-language in English is widespread, this is not necessarily the case in all language contexts. To anticipate the challenges that might be faced when building the e-language element of CorCenCC, and to inform the procedures to be used in the collation of this sub-corpus, a 500,000-word pilot corpus was built in 2013.

Bloggers/sites on 'popular' or 'top-ten' lists were targeted for the pilot (e.g. 'Welsh bloggers' on Wikipedia). This was to ensure that the content was likely to be read by a critical mass of Welsh speakers, to represent the typical online language Welsh speakers are exposed to in their day-to-day lives. Lists of 'popular' Welsh Tweeters proved more difficult to find and a single source (http://indigenoustweets.com/cy/) provided the main point of reference for targeting contributors. As well as being listed on this site, the majority of the targeted Tweeters also had over 500 followers, again suggesting that the content is representative of what one would expect from the Welsh language online.

Potential contributors were then contacted via email, outlining the aims and objectives of the pilot, and requesting permission from the authors to use their data in the dataset (for a more detailed discussion of participant recruitment and data collection strategies, see Chapter 3). Eighty blog users and 80 Tweeters were contacted, with 42 of the former and 32 of the latter providing full permission to harvest their data. This level of uptake was encouraging, indicating that there is a certain level of community pride and engagement coupled with an interest in sustaining and 'growing' the language thereby suggesting that the plan to develop an e-language component in CorCenCC (and indeed the wider corpus), was a viable one. This finding also motivated the use of the crowdsourcing approach for data collection in this project (see Chapter 3).

The pilot comprised the following data:

- **Blogs**: 42 contributors; 807 posts; 257,658 words
- **Tweets**: 32 contributors; 14,630 posts; 271,650 words
  - **Total** = 74 contributors; 15,437 posts; 529,308 words

As was seen in the development of CANELC (above), there is a considerable discrepancy between the number of posts across the two genres here (with a less significant difference in word count). There was also variability across individual contributors, the lengths of the texts they posted and the frequency with which they posted them. This indicated that contribution-to-length distribution, and likely individual variability of contributions need careful consideration when designing and building e-language corpora. These findings were fed directly into the development of CorCenCC's final e-language design frame discussed below.

The next finding from the pilot study was that the e-language data collected covered a range of thematic categories, which could be classified according to an adapted version of the taxonomy utilised by CANELC. Consequently, the following additions were made to the original taxonomy:

- 'History and religion' to category B
- 'Gigs and events' to category D

While the assignment of the content to the thematic groupings was transparent in some cases, other texts were more challenging to categorise as they discussed multiple topics ranging across the different categories. In these instances, the data was given a range of category codes, e.g. 'A/B/C' rather than simply 'A'. Twenty-six texts were classified under thematic category A, 34 under B, 10 under C, 17 under D, five under E and 36 under F. All the categories were represented in the pilot, so a good range of different topics was provided by the dataset (although categories A and F had the highest word counts). The CANELC coding scheme was considered fit-for-purpose as a broad guideline for classifying e-language texts in CorCenCC, although changes/tweaks to this scheme would likely be required when building a more extensive dataset.

There was wide variability in the biographical metadata of contributors to the pilot. This highlighted to the team that while there is the potential for collecting e-language data from a broad demographic of individuals, the likelihood of being able to provide any 'balance' across these would be minimal. This finding informed the broader design principle for CorCenCC which although seeking to include speakers from a representative range of ages, occupations and genders located in different geographical regions of Wales, across different language varieties (regional and social), data collection would not be restricted by this aim. Rather than utilising a 'demographic approach' to data collection (see above), a context/genre-driven approach was to be used.

Albeit fairly small scale and restricted to a single mode of language (i.e. e-language), the findings discussed here underline the significant value that the piloting of the development of a corpus can bring. This is relevant to the final question:

> 5. In what ways might be it be useful to pilot the development of a corpus?

The development of a pilot corpus in your own language, including data of *any* mode, is also advisable as it will help tease out some of the key challenges and context-specific affordances that are likely to be faced when a more extensive project is embarked upon.

Sampling and Categorising Welsh e-Language

In this section, the final design frame developed for CorCenCC's e-language sub-corpus is presented.

Data in CorCenCC's e-language sub-corpus aimed to represent language that exists, and has been produced, in an online environment only (i.e. not written texts that have been reproduced online). In terms of the specific *genres* of e-language to be targeted, blogs were first explored. The frequency with which bloggers post contributions is often highly variable, with some personal blogs being updated sporadically while others are regularly updated and contain thousands of posts. Blogs also vary in their length of contributions, running 'from a few sentences to numerous paragraphs of text' (Knight et al., 2014: 40). This variability poses some challenges when building corpora as striking a balance in the number of words and amount of blog entries contributed across different blog sites can be difficult. The initial target set for this genre was 30% (600,000 words) of the entire e-language sub-corpus due to the predominance of blog texts online.

It is useful, when revisiting the question (in relation to e-language specifically)…:

> **3.** What resources and/or information can be examined as a means of setting data collection targets for corpora?

…to identify, first, which specific blog sites to target. The requirements used in the creation of CANELC can be used (Knight et al., 2014: 35–36):

- sites had to feature within online directories of the most popular blog/Tweet lists (sourced by Googling 'top ten blogs', 'popular blogs' and so on)
- posts from blogging sites had either a range of readers/followers and/or numerous responses to posts, indicating a large readership

To facilitate this in the context of CorCenCC, various popular blogging sites (e.g. blogger.com and wordpress.com) acted as a useful starting point, along with blog collation sites (including the Welsh-language focused http://www.blogiadur.com/—now defunct). Each targeted site was to be public rather than private, with individual site owners contacted and asked for their permission for data to be extracted/collected for use in the corpus.

Regarding websites, of the 2200 people who responded to the National Survey for Wales 2016–2017, 36% indicated that they had viewed a website in the Welsh language in the month prior to responding (National Survey Team, 2016). This suggests that Welsh-language websites are well used by Welsh speakers, justifying why this genre should represent a large proportion of the sub-corpus. As with blogs, the initial target set for this genre was 30% of the sub-corpus (600,000 words).

There was also an aim to target sites that had received a large number of visitors, as detailed by www.similarweb.com (a site that allows users to view traffic data for other websites), but to balance the selection of these business-facing, public and/or corporate websites with more localised and individual sites. While a smaller website's text was to be collected in its entirety, only a proportional sample of larger sites was to be harvested for use, following a similar strategy to that proposed for large books.

Although there was a provisional plan to include language data from discussion boards in CorCenCC (Table 2.1), extensive online searches indicated that only four discussion boards/forums conducted through the medium of Welsh were in existence at the time. Of these, three had been dormant for many years. The inactive status of this data type in the Welsh language meant that it was removed from the design frame.

Twitter and other social media sites are well used in the Welsh-language context and, consequently, were considered desirable sources of data to include. However, unlike the pilot corpus which was not intended to be published or made accessible to anyone beyond the research team (it was built solely to help articulate some of the challenges to be faced when building a more extensive dataset), CorCenCC was always intended as an open-source dataset. At the time of planning CorCenCC, Twitter's 'rules of the road' (Twitter, 2012—website now defunct) stated that it was not permissible to distribute Tweets outside of the Twitter platform. This lack of compatibility with the aims of CorCenCC meant that this data could not be included. Similar issues regarding access and permissions for data distribution and re-use also meant that content from other SNSs such as Facebook was also not included in CorCenCC's revised design frame. However, the additional inclusion of this data would be invaluable should distribution/permission requirements change in the future (for further discussions on ethics in corpus building, see Chapter 3).

For more personal forms of e-language (emails, SMSs), there is a disparity between the number of these messages communicated in Welsh compared to English, even among Welsh speakers (Beaufort Research, 2013: 28). Only 42% of Welsh-speaking respondents to the Beaufort Research survey, a survey that profiles life in Wales, had sent a Welsh-language email in the previous month, with 72% having sent at least one in English. Furthermore, 44% of respondents had sent a Welsh-language SMS in the previous month (Beaufort Research, 2013: 28–31). These reported patterns of usage, along with the well-documented diffi-culties associated with collecting email and SMS data (Hawtin, 2018;

Knight et al., 2014; Tagg, 2009, among others), meant that the original targets for collecting these forms of data were set at just 20% each (400,000 words each) of the overall sub-corpus.

There was also an aim to target the collection of emails based on their communicative purpose, and whether they fulfilled 'personal' or 'business'-related functions. These classifications crudely align with the spoken sub-corpus design frame with business messages likely to be 'transactional' or 'professional' in nature, and personal messages more akin to 'socialising' or 'private' communication. It seemed likely that business email messages would be more plentiful than personal ones, so the targets for these genres were designed with this in mind (with two-thirds dedicated to the former and one third to the latter).

Each e-language text was to be categorised in respect of its 'topic', defined as the 'aboutness/thematic focus of the text'. Table 2.12 details the revised design frame for CorCenCC's e-language data. As mentioned above, the initial aim was to use the thematic framework provided in CANELC (Knight et al., 2014) as a guiding principle for categorisation, although as some major language categories don't always correspond to minoritised/minority language domains and categories, some modifications were required to ensure it was appropriate for use in the Welsh-language context.

For instance, religion was not included as a category in CANELC; however, religion is an important historical domain in Welsh. 10% of blogs posted on the Welsh-language blog collation site www.blogiadur.com (now defunct) over a four-day period (12–16 April 2016) were religious in nature. 'Religion', then, needed to be included as a topic in CorCenCC. Regarding CANELC's categories of 'fashion' and 'health and beauty', the developers of CorCenCC felt it more appropriate for 'health' to be a distinct category of its own. By using the label 'health and beauty', any e-language text discussing cancer or any illness would be assigned to the same category as a text discussing hair care products or general grooming, which seemed inappropriate. To mitigate this, 'health and beauty' was renamed 'health and wellbeing', with 'beauty' included with 'fashion'. Finally, as goods are now often purchased online, an additional context, 'online shopping' was added to group A. Language is an oft-discussed topic in Wales and is an important part of the Welsh cultural identity, so a 'language' category was also created.

Table 2.12 Design frame for e-language data in CorCenCC

Genre	Topic(s)	Words (target)	% e-language sub-corpus	Total
Blog	News, media and current affairs, politics, business and finance, weather and the environment, online shopping	100,000	5%	600,000 [30%]
	Religion, language, culture, literature and the arts, teaching, academia, and education	100,000	5%	
	Technology, computers and gaming, fashion and beauty, hobbies and pastimes, travel, cookery	100,000	5%	
	Music, sport, gigs, and events	100,000	5%	
	Celebrity news and gossip, TV and film, humour	100,000	5%	
	Parenting and family life, health and wellbeing, personal and daily life	100,000	5%	
Website	News, media and current affairs, politics, business and finance, weather and the environment, online shopping	100,000	5%	600,000 [30%]
	Religion, language, culture, literature and the arts, teaching, academia, and education	100,000	5%	
	Technology, computers and gaming, fashion and beauty, hobbies and pastimes, travel, cookery	100,000	5%	
	Music, sport, gigs, and events	100,000	5%	
	Celebrity news and gossip, TV and film, humour	100,000	5%	
	Parenting and family life, health and wellbeing, personal and daily life	100,000	5%	
Email	Private	132,000	6.6%	400,000 [20%]
	Professional	268,000	13.4%	
SMS		400,000	20%	400,000 [20%]
			100%	2,000,000

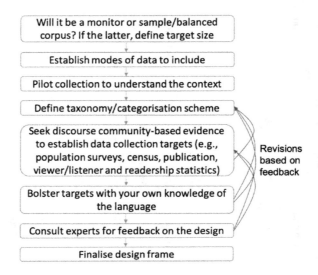

Fig. 2.1 Workflow for creating corpus design frames

Summary

Using a case study approach, this chapter has provided a demonstration of how a detailed design frame for a national corpus may be built. Focusing on each individual 'mode' of data in turn, the chapter has explored some of the key generic questions that are helpful in guiding design frame development, questions that may be adapted for use in other language contexts. Figure 2.1 provides a workflow for the creation of design frames (relevant to all modes), based on this chapter.

At this stage, the following question arises: now that I have a plan for my corpus in place, what steps do I need to take to ensure that this plan comes to fruition? The next two chapters aim to answer this question, starting, in Chapter 3, with a detailed exploration of the different approaches to participant recruitment and data collection.

References

Aroonmanakun, W., Tansiri, K., & Nittayanuparp, P. (2009). Thai National Corpus: A progress report. Proceedings of the *7th Workshop on Asian Language Resources (ALR7)*, Suntec, Singapore, pp. 153–158.

Asheghi, N. R., Sharoff, S., & Markert, K. (2016). Crowdsourcing for web genre annotation. *Language Resources and Evaluation, 50*(3), 603–641.

Asheghi, N., S., & Markert, K. (2014). Designing and evaluating a reliable corpus of web genres via crowd-sourcing. Proceedings of the *Language Resources and Evaluation Conference*, Reykjavik: Iceland, pp. 1339–1346.

Aston, G., & Burnard, L. (1997). *The BNC handbook: Exploring the British National Corpus with SARA*. Edinburgh University Press.

Atkins, S., Clear, J., & Ostler, N. (1992). Corpus design criteria. *Literary and Linguistic Computing, 7*(1), 1–16.

Beaufort Research. (2013). *Ymchwilio i ddefnydd iaith siaradwyr Cymraeg yn eu bywyd pob dydd* [*Exploring Welsh speakers' language use in their daily lives*] [Online]. Retrieved from https://www.s4c.cymru/abouts4c/corporate/pdf/e_daily-lives-and-language-use-research-report.pdf. Accessed 20 June 2021.

Biber, D. (1994). Representativeness in corpus design. In A. Zampolli, N. Calzolari, & M. Palmer (Eds.), *Current issues in computational linguistics: In Honour of Don Walker* (pp.377–407). Dordrecht: Springer Netherlands.

Biber, D., & Egbert, J. (2018). *Register variation online*. Cambridge University Press.

Biber, D., Egbert, J., & Davies, M. (2015). Exploring the composition of the searchable web: A corpus-based taxonomy of web registers. *Corpora, 10*(1), 11–45.

Bible Society. (1997). *Challenge to change: Results of the 1995 Welsh churches survey*. Bible Society.

Burnard, L. (2007). *Reference guide for the British national corpus* (XML Edition). Retrieved from: http://www.natcorp.ox.ac.uk/docs/URG/index.html. Accessed 20 June 2021.

Carter, R. (1998). Orders of reality: CANCODE, communication, and culture. *ELT Journal, 52*(1), 43–56.

Carter, R., & McCarthy, M. (2004). Talking, creating: Interactional language, creativity, and context. *Applied Linguistics, 25*(1), 62–88.

Cheng, W., & Warren, M. (1999). Facilitating a description of intercultural conversations: The Hong Kong Corpus of Conversational English. *International Computer Archive of Modern English, 20*, 5–20.

Coleg Cymraeg Cenedlaethol [National Welsh College]. (2014). *Circular: 2015/16 Welsh medium targets*. Retrieved from http://www.colegcymraeg.ac.uk/en/media/main/dogfennau-ccc/cylchlythyron/REF14_1TargetCircular.pdf. Accessed 20 June 2021.

Condon, S., & Cech, C. (1996). Functional comparison of face-to-face and computer- mediated decision-making interactions. In S. Herring (Ed.), *Computer-mediated communication: Linguistic, social, and cross-cultural perspectives* (pp.65–80). John Benjamins.

Crowdy, S. (1993). Spoken corpus design. *Literary and Linguistic Computing, 8*, 259–265.

Crystal, D. (2008). Texting. *ELT Journal, 62*(1), 77–83.

CUP. (2020). *Cambridge English corpus* [Online]. Retrieved from https://www.cambridge.org/us/cambridgeenglish/better-learning-insights/corpus. Accessed 20 June 2021.

Cymdeithas yr Iaith Gymraeg [Welsh Language Society]. (2015). *Herio Aelodau Cynulliad: Gwnewch adduned blwyddyn newydd i siarad mwy o Gymraeg yn 2016* [Challenging Assembly Members: Make a new year's resolution to speak more Welsh in 2016]. Retrieved from http://cymdeithas.cymru/new yddion/herio-aelodau-cynulliad-gwnewch-adduned-blwyddyn-newydd-i-sia rad-mwy-o-gymraeg-yn-2016. Accessed 20 June 2021.

Davies, M. (2010). The corpus of contemporary American English as the first reliable monitor corpus of English. *Literary and Linguistic Computing, 25*(4), 447–464.

Davies, M. (2016). *Corpus of news on the web (NOW)* [Online]. Retrieved from https://www.english-corpora.org/now/. Accessed 20 June 2021.

Davies, M., & Fuchs, R. (2015). Expanding horizons in the study of World Englishes with the 1.9 billion word Global Web-based English Corpus (GloWbE). *English World-Wide, 36*(1), 1–28.

Eisteddfod Genedlaethol Cymru [National Eisteddfod of Wales]. (2016). *Ffigurau Ymwelwyr yr Wythnos* [*The week's visitor figures*]. Retrieved from https://eisteddfod.cymru/ffigurau-ymwelwyr-yr-wythnos. Accessed 20 June 2021.

Ferraresi, A., Zanchetta, E., Bernardini, S., & Baroni, M. (2008). Introducing and evaluating ukWaC, a very large Web-derived corpus of English. Proceedings of the *4th Web as Corpus Workshop (WAC-4)*, Marrakech, Morocco, pp.47–54.

Forsyth, E., & Martell, C. (2007). Lexical and discourse analysis of online chat dialog. Proceedings of the *International Conference on Semantic Computing (ICSC 2007)*, Irvine, California, pp.19–26.

Gardner, S., & Moreton, E. (2020). Written corpora. In S. Adolphs & D. Knight (Eds.), *The Routledge handbook of English language and digital humanities* (pp. 26–48). Routledge.

Gries, S. T., & Newman, J. (2014). Creating and using corpora. In D. Sharma & R. J. Podesva (Eds.), *Research methods in linguistics* (pp. 257–287). Cambridge University Press.

Gwales.com. (2012). *Gwales.com*. Retrieved from www.gwales.com. Accessed 20 June 2021.

Halliday, M. A. K. (1978). *Language as social semiotic: The social interpretation of language and meaning*. Edward Arnold.

Handford, M. (2010). *The language of business meetings.* Cambridge University Press.

Hawtin, A. (2018). *The written British national corpus 2014: Design, compilation and analysis* [Unpublished PhD Thesis]. Lancaster University, Lancaster.

Heer, J., & Boyd, D. (2005). Vizster: Visualizing online social networks. Proceedings of the *IEEE Symposium on Information Visualization (INFOVIS 2005)*, Minneapolis, pp.32–39.

Herring, S. C. (2007). A faceted classification scheme for computer-mediated discourse. *Language@Internet, 4*(1), 1–37.

Hughes, S. (2015). *School census results, 2015: First release* [Online]. Retrieved from: https://gov.wales/sites/default/files/statistics-and-research/2019-05/school-census-results-2015.pdf. Accessed 20 June 2021.

Hunston, S. (2008). Collection strategies and design decisions. In A. Lüdeling & M. Kytö (Eds.), *Corpus linguistics: An international handbook* (pp. 154–168). de Gruyter.

Jakubíček, M., Kilgarriff, A., Kovář, V., Rychlý, P., & Suchomel, V. (2013). The tenten corpus family. Paper presented at the *The 7th International Corpus Linguistics Conference*, Lancaster University, UK.

Johansson, S., Leech, G., & Goodluck, H. (1978). *Manual of information to accompany the Lancaster-Oslo/Bergen corpus of British English, for use with digital computers–Technical report.* University of Oslo.

Kilgarriff, A., Reddy, S., Pomikálek, J., & Pvs, A. (2010). A Corpus factory for many languages. Proceedings of the *Language Resources and Evaluation (LREC)*, Valetta, Malta, pp.904–910.

Kirk, J., & Nelson, G. (2018). The international corpus of English project: A progress report. *World Englishes, 37*(4), 697–716.

Klimt, B., & Yang, Y. (2004). Introducing the enron corpus. Proceedings of the *European Conference on Machine Learning (ECML)*, Pisa, Italy, pp. 217–226.

Knight, D. (2015). e-Language: Communication in the Digital Age. In T. McEnery & P. Baker (Eds.), *Corpora and discourse studies—Integrating discourse and corpora* (pp. 20–40). Palgrave.

Knight, D., Adolphs, S., & Carter, R. (2014). CANELC—Constructing an e-language corpus. *Corpora, 9*(1), 29–56.

Knight, D., Bayoumi, S., Mills, S., Crabtree, A., Adolphs, S., Pridmore, T., & Carter, R. (2006). Beyond the text: Construction and analysis of multi-modal linguistic corpora. Paper presented at the *2nd International Conference on e-Social Science*, Manchester.

Knight, D., Morris, S., & Fitzpatrick, T. (2021). *Corpus design and construction in minoritised language contexts: The national corpus of contemporary Welsh.* Palgrave.

Ko, K. (1996). Structural characteristics of computer-mediated language: A comparative analysis of InterChange discourse. *Electronic Journal of Communication, 6*(3).

Lee, D. Y. W. (2001). Genres, registers, text types, domains and styles: Clarifying the concepts and navigating a path through the BNC jungle. *Language Learning and Technology, 5*, 37–72.

Lleol.net. (2014). *The directory of Welsh language service providers* [Online]. Retrieved from http://www.lleol.cymru/en/listing/. Accessed 20 June 2021.

Love, R. (2020). *Overcoming challenges in corpus construction*. Routledge.

Love, R., Dembry, C., Hardie, A., Brezina, V., & McEnery, T. (2017). The spoken BNC2014: Designing and building a spoken corpus of everyday conversations. *International Journal of Corpus Linguistics, 22*, 319–344.

Love, R., Hawtin, A., & Hardie, A. (2017). *The British National Corpus 2014: User manual and reference guide (version 1.0)*. Retrieved from: http://corpora.lancs.ac.uk/bnc2014/doc/BNC2014manual.pdf. Accessed 20 June 2021.

McCarthy, M. J. (1998). *Spoken language and applied linguistics*. Cambridge University Press.

McEnery, T., Xiao, R., & Tono, Y. (2006). *Corpus-based language studies an advanced resource book*. Routledge.

National Survey Team (Welsh Government). (2016). *Results viewer—Viewed websites in Welsh in the last month*. Retrieved from https://gov.wales/national-survey-wales-results-viewer. Accessed 20 June 2021.

National Survey Team (Welsh Government). (2015). *Welsh language use survey 2013–15: Use of the Welsh language*. Retrieved from: https://statswales.gov.wales/Download/File?fileId=507. Accessed 20 June 2021.

Nelson, F. W., & Kucera, H. (1967). *Computational analysis of present-day American English*. Brown University Press.

Ofcom. (2015). *The UK is now a smartphone society* [Online]. Retrieved from http://media.ofcom.org.uk/news/2015/cmr-uk-2015/. Accessed 20 June 2021.

ONS (Office for National Statistics). (2011). *Census: Digitised boundary data (England and Wales)* [Computer File]. Retrieved from https://borders.ukdataservice.ac.uk/. Accessed 20 June 2021.

Rajar. (2016). *Quarterly summary of radio listening: Survey period ending 20th December 2015* [Online]. Retrieved from http://www.rajar.co.uk/docs/2015_12/2015_Q4_Quarterly_Summary_Figures.pdf. Accessed 20 June 2021.

Reppen, R. (2010). Building a COrpus. In A. O'Keeffe & M. J. McCarthy (Eds.), *The Routledge handbook of corpus linguistics* (pp. 31–37). Routledge.

Rosser, S. (2012). Language, culture and identity in Welsh children's literature: O.M. Edwards and Cymru'r Plant 1892–1920. In N. Congáil (Ed.),

Codladh Céad Bliain: Cnuasach Aistí ar Litríocht na nÓg (pp. 223–251). LeabhairCOMHAR.

S4C. (2015). *Annual report & statement of accounts for the 12 month period to 31 March 2015* [Online]. Retrieved from http://www.s4c.cymru/abouts4c/annualreport/acrobats/s4c-annual-report-2015.pdf. Accessed 20 June 2021.

S4C. (2016). *Amserlenni [Timetables]*. Retrieved from http://www.s4c.cymru/c_listings.shtml?dt=2016-04-27. Accessed 20 June 2021.

Schler, J., Koppel, M., Argamon, S., & Pennebaker, J. (2006). Effects of age and gender on blogging. Paper presented at the *2006 AAAI Spring Symposium on Computational Approaches for Analyzing Weblogs*, Palo Alto, California.

Siepmann, D., Bürgel, C., & Sascha, D. (2015). The Corpus de référence du français contemporain (CRFC) as the first genre-diverse mega-corpus of French. *International Journal of Lexicography, 30*(1), 63–84.

Simpson, R., Lucka, B., & Ovens, J. (2000). Methodological challenges of planning a spoken corpus with pedagogic outcomes. In L. Burnard & T. McEnery (Eds.), *Rethinking language pedagogy from a corpus perspective: Papers from the Third International Conference on Teaching and Language Corpora* (pp. 43–49). Lang.

Sinclair, J. (1987). Collocation: A progress report. In R. Steele & T. Threadgold (Eds.), *Language topics: Essays in honour of Michael Halliday* (pp. 319–331). John Benjamins.

Sinclair, J. (1991). *Corpus, concordance, collocation*. Oxford University Press.

Stubbe, A., Ringlstetter, C., & Schulz, K. (2007). Genre as noise: Noise in genre. *International Journal on Document Analysis and Recognition, 10*, 199–209.

Tagg, C. (2009). *A corpus linguistics study of SMS text messaging* [Unpublished PhD Thesis]. Birmingham: University of Birmingham.

Thompson, P., & Nesi, H. (2001). The British Academic Spoken English (BASE) corpus project. *Language Teaching Research, 5*, 263–264.

Twitter. (2012). *API Terms of Service: between Sept 5, 2012 and July 2, 2013* [Online]. Retrieved from https://dev.twitter.com/archive/terms/api-terms/diff-20130702. Accessed 11 June 2014.

Urdd Gobaith Cymru. (2021). *What is the Eisteddfod*. Retrieved from https://www.urdd.cymru/en/eisteddfod/what-eisteddfod/.

Welsh Books Council. (2012). *Buying and reading Welsh-language books: Welsh Speakers Omnibus Survey 2012—Report of survey findings*. Retrieved from https://llyfrau.cymru/wp-content/uploads/2021/01/Buying_and_Reading_Welsh-language_Books_-_Welsh_Speakers_Omnibus_Survey_2012_-_July_2013.pdf. Accessed 20 June 2021.

Welsh Government (StatsWales). (2015). *Further education: Learning activities at further education institutions by subject and medium of delivery: 2012/13* [Online]. Retrieved from https://statswales.gov.wales/Catalogue/Education-and-Skills/Post-16-Education-and-Training/Further-Education-and-Work-Based-Learning/Learners/Further-Education/learningactivitiesfurthereducationinstitutions-by-subject-mediumofdelivery. Accessed 20 June 2021.

WJEC (Welsh Joint Education Committee). (2012). *Final results archive* [Online]. Retrieved from http://www.wjec.co.uk/students/results-and-research/results-statistics.html. Accessed 20 June 2021.

WJEC (Welsh Joint Education Committee). (2015). *Results statistics: Welsh medium entries* [Online]. Retrieved from http://www.wjec.co.uk/students/results-and-research/results-statistics.html. Accessed 20 June 2021.

Yiğit, O. (2005). *Emoticon usage in task-oriented and socio-emotional contexts in online discussion boards* [Unpublished PhD Thesis]. Florida State University, Florida.

CHAPTER 3

(Meta)Data Collection

Abstract Together with a consideration of the general types of text/data to be included in a corpus (as examined by the development of the design frames in Chapter 2), attention needs to be given to *who* will contribute data and *how* they will be recruited. This chapter focuses specifically on the stages of participant recruitment and (meta)data collection when building a corpus. Drawing on our experience in sourcing and collecting the (meta)data for CorCenCC, the contents of this chapter are scaffolded by some important central generic questions that are relevant to anyone wanting to build a corpus in a minoritised/under-resourced, or indeed any, language.

Keywords Data collection · Crowdsourcing · OCR · Metadata · Language champions · Ethics · Anonymity · Participant/contributor recruitment

OVERVIEWS

Once the principled design frame(s) for a corpus has been developed, the next stage of the corpus building process is to establish approaches to contributor recruitment and the collection of both the language data and 'data about the data' (i.e. metadata). Drawing on the experience of

© The Author(s), under exclusive license to Springer Nature Switzerland AG 2021
D. Knight et al., *Building a National Corpus*,
https://doi.org/10.1007/978-3-030-81858-6_3

75

building CorCenCC, the contents of this chapter are scaffolded by some important central generic questions that are relevant to anyone wanting to build a corpus in a minoritised/under-resourced, or indeed any, language, including:

1. What approaches can be used to recruit participants/contributors to a corpus?
2. Which file formats are easiest to collect/process for inclusion in a corpus?
3. What is the quickest and most efficient way of collecting e-language?
4. How can crowdsourcing techniques be usefully applied as a data collection method?
5. What forms of metadata exist and how can this information be obtained from participants/contributors to a corpus?
6. What are some of the key ethical issues and challenges that should be considered before collecting data for a corpus?
7. When and why might it be appropriate to modify/change corpus data?

Participant Recruitment

Together with a consideration of the general types of text/data to be included in a corpus, attention needs to be given to *who* will contribute data and *how* they will be recruited. 'Participants' (or 'contributors') may be specific individuals and/or groups, professional organisations, companies and so on.

1. What approaches can be used to recruit participants/contributors to a corpus?

In response to this question, participants can first be drawn in by advertising to specific communities (via mailshots, posters, social media campaigns) or at a national level through media campaigns. To both raise the profile and awareness of the project and to attract potential participants/contributors to CorCenCC, promotional materials were created and distributed to the wider speech community. This included the creation of a bilingual project website, Twitter and Facebook accounts and the production of leaflets, coasters (Fig. 3.1), postcards and pens. Members of the team also appeared on various media outlets, for example in items in national TV and radio news programmes (Welsh and English-medium), as well as in informal daytime 'magazine' programmes (such as *Prynhawn da* on S4C) to promote the project/corpus (see Knight et al., 2021: 44–52 for the conceptual user-driven design used to underpin this).

Developers of the *Siarad* corpus also discuss the benefit of drawing on personal contacts, that is, friends of friends, offline social networks, students, colleagues and local community members to aid participant recruitment (Deuchar et al., 2018). When sourcing participants for CorCenCC, then, the team also looked for an entry point that could offer representative access to likely candidates in the speech community. To that end, organisations directly linked to the support of the Welsh language were contacted, including *Mentrau Iaith Cymru*, the umbrella body that

Fig. 3.1 Promotional coaster used to recruit contributors to the CorCenCC corpus

supports a network of local *Mentrau Iaith* (Welsh-language initiatives—singular *Menter Iaith*) throughout Wales. Each local authority area in Wales has a *Menter Iaith* assigned to it, although some *Mentrau Iaith* are responsible for more than one local authority, and sometimes more than one *Menter Iaith* exists within a single authority. Consequently, the *Mentrau Iaith* were considered to be best placed to provide information on local Welsh-language groups and events and to effect introductions that would facilitate, in particular, the collection of spoken Welsh. The principled geographical spread of the *Mentrau Iaith* also helped to ensure that the multiple dialects of Wales were adequately captured in the corpus.

The idea of using a locally based *pencampwr* (champion) was also developed to further extend the reach and cover of the data collected. These *pencampwyr* (champions) were individuals who were typically (but not uniquely) identified through contact with the *Mentrau Iaith* and were recognised members of their communities, closely identified with the Welsh language and its use in varied domains in the locality. They would facilitate onward contact with participants whom it might otherwise have proved difficult to recruit.

In addition to these, more targeted approaches to recruitment were also used for some of the contributors of written and e-language data. Direct contact was, for example, made with publishers of Welsh-language books and journals, who gave permission for many thousands of words of published Welsh to be collected. The work involved in establishing this sort of agreement, however, should not be underestimated and often involves more time than might be initially anticipated. Blog writers and website owners of popular public-facing sites (i.e. those with a wide readership), for example, were also contacted directly (via email or instant message) and asked for permission for their data to be used.

Data Collection

In any project, once potential participants/contributors have been identified, there are several methods of acquiring texts in a form that could be used to create a corpus. Conventionally, texts in corpora are stored as .txt files. Saving your own corpus files in a consistent/standardised way enables the data to be reused by others (for a more detailed discussion of file formats at every stage of the corpus building process, see Gries & Newman, 2014). For CorCenCC, .txt files with utf-8 encoding were required as this encoding preserved Welsh-language characters in the texts. Other language contexts may have specific encoding requirements that the corpus developers must ensure they are aware of.

> **2. Which file formats are easiest to collect/process for inclusion in a corpus?**

In response to the second question, written texts that are available in an already digital form, particularly those that are available as .txt or .doc files require relatively minimal processing before they can be added to a corpus. Texts available as formatted documents including PDFs require converting and checking before they can be used. Given this, the aim was to include .txt and .doc files for use in CorCenCC in the first instance. Not all written texts that corpus developers might want to include are in such convenient formats, however, such as hard copies of paper-based documents (printed or handwritten) and/or published books. In these cases, corpus builders are faced with a primary challenge of digitising the texts. This is typically undertaken using OCR (Optical Character Recognition) technology.

In some major languages including English, OCR technologies provide accurate results in digitising texts and have become a mainstay for use in corpus building. OCR was, for example, used in the development of the BNC 1994 and the Written BNC 2014. Drawing on the PPSR approach (Public Participation in Scientific Research, Shirk et al., 2012—discussed below), the Written BNC2014 team recruited (and paid) volunteers to manually scan excerpts from texts that they had legal access to (i.e. texts the volunteers had purchased), before submitting them for inclusion in the corpus (Hawtin, 2018). This approach helped to quickly amass a large number of written texts, so is useful for others to consider replicating when creating their own corpus. OCR was also used in the development of the Swiss Alpine Club heritage corpus of German and French (Clematide et al., 2016). The scanned texts in this corpus were also checked by volunteers via a crowdsourcing approach.

As seen in Chapter 1, OCR technology is not compatible with the characters used in some languages, so cannot read and digitise them effectively (e.g. $\hat{W}/\hat{w}$ and $\hat{Y}/\hat{y}$ in Welsh). The possible utility of OCR with

Welsh was assessed, but the level of accuracy was found to be relatively low. This meant that additional time would be required to manually check data. The cost (in time and resources) of this OCR approach was seen to outweigh the potential benefit offered by it. Granted, there would have been an option to draw on the 'crowd' of Welsh-language contributors to help with this task, but it was felt that the crowd's time would be better spent recording the spoken conversation or offering up their own digitally based texts for inclusion instead.

The approach used to extract written data, then, depended on the format in which the data was received. Again, ideally texts would be received as .txt files or .doc documents that could subsequently be converted into .txt. It was common, however, for PDF files to be received. These required further conversion. The use of AntFileConverter (Anthony, 2017) and other PDF conversion packages to undertake this process was tested, but due to some issues relating to the encoding of the documents, the conversions created extensive non-recoverable errors with non-ASCII characters such as $ŷ$ and $ẃ$ and other even more widely used diacritics. The time taken to fix these errors would have been substantial. A more manually based approach was therefore used, whereby each PDF was:

   i. Opened in Word
  ii. Saved as a .txt utf-8 file
 iii. Opened in a text and code editing tool
 iv. Corrected using an automated script (i.e. computer code/software) where possible, and then by hand
  v. Saved again before specific excerpts of the text were sampled/extracted for use.

3. What is the quickest and most efficient way of collecting e-language?

The proliferation of user-generated content (e.g. blogs, websites) online provides opportunities for the use of technologically sophisticated methods to automatically obtain large quantities of e-language data without having to, for example, key in or scan in documents. Web-scraping refers to the process of automatically extracting information from online resources. Web-scrapers are built using text-based mark-up languages that automatically strip/extract texts from digital resources using an API (Application Programming Interface), and automatically store this content as a .txt file.

Web-scraping is common to corpus building, and was used to build some Sketch Engine corpora, the *An Crúbadán* corpora (Scannell, 2007) and CUCWeb (Boleda et al., 2006). Using, for example, the blog collation sites and information on popular Welsh-language websites and aligning these with the design frame in Table 2.12, specific site owners and/or potential contributors to the e-language sub-corpus were contacted directly. Consent and speaker/author information forms were then sent to those who responded positively. Once fully signed consent forms were received, Python, a high-level programming language, was used to implement a web-scraper to automatically retrieve and clean the Welsh e-language resources (based on their URLs). This approach was relevant to both blogs and websites and was adapted for use when extracting email texts. IMs (i.e. instant messages/text messages) were sent directly from contributors to a project mobile phone before they were individually (and automatically) extracted to a computer, anonymised and checked and finally saved as .txt files.

Regarding spoken data, the project's research assistants were first tasked with attending relevant Welsh-language events etc., and manually recording data in situ. This was carried out using digital recorders and/or mobile phones, once appropriate procedures for data collection had been ratified by the project team, and then only when full permission had been received from participants. It would not be ethical to simply record conversations without permission (ethical considerations need to be in place in advance and these are discussed in more detail later in this chapter). When 'on location', the researchers briefed potential participants on the project and recording process and gave them ample opportunity to ask any questions that they might have. If/when permission was granted for recordings to take place, the researcher either directly used the recording devices (i.e. pressing record and moving to the back of the room to prevent any interference with the flow of communication) or left devices with consenting participants to operate. Recording devices were also left in shops, with signs to alert customers to the fact recordings were taking place and informing them of what to do if they preferred their recordings not be used in the final corpus dataset (Appendix 1). In addition, contributors were given project information sheets, including contact details for the researcher(s), after the recording had taken place (Appendix 2).

To complement this more traditional approach to data collection, a key innovation of the CorCenCC project was to experiment with a potential future method of corpus compilation: a system for enabling user-generated 'live' spoken and written data collection via crowdsourcing. This is relevant to question four:

> 4. How can crowdsourcing techniques be usefully applied as a data collection method?

Crowdsourcing is a method of outsourcing specific tasks to large groups and/or the general public (the *crowd*). While the term crowdsourcing was coined in 2005 (Howe, 2006), this community-based, cooperative approach has a long history, with perhaps the earliest example being the development of the 1857 edition of the New Oxford English Dictionary (which received over 6-million submissions following the editor's public call for contributions).

Modern crowdsourcing methods draw on a more extensive online and digital 'crowd'. They have been used for a range of purposes from raising funds for product development, charities and business ventures (e.g. GoFundMe, Kickstarter, JustGiving), and are at the core of the encyclopaedia website, Wikipedia. There are three main types of crowdsourcing approach: 'paid-for crowdsourcing, games with a purpose, volunteering-based approaches' (Sabou et al., 2014: 859). In the first, contributors are reimbursed for their time, while the second (games with a purpose, GWAP, see Adda et al., 2014) focuses on providing contributors with tasks that are 'fun' and/or competitive. Altruism and the goodwill of individuals lie at the heart of volunteering-based approaches.

There is an increasing amount of applied linguistic research that utilises crowdsourcing methods, including for the annotation of datasets (Asheghi et al., 2014), training of speech recognition systems (McGraw et al., 2009), transcription (Gruenstein et al., 2009) and data collection, particularly when sourcing dialect data (Caines et al., 2016). Compared to the hard sciences, however, this approach is still relatively underused, particularly in the case of building spoken corpora. A noteworthy exception to this was the 'national participation campaign' (Love et al., 2017: 320) based on 'Public Participation in Scientific Research' (PPSR, Shirk et al., 2012), an approach akin to crowdsourcing, that was used in the creation of the Spoken BNC2014. Here, anyone interested in participating signed up via the project website and was then asked to record their own conversations using their mobile phone before submitting their recordings, consent forms and metadata information to the project team. Contributors were then reimbursed at a rate of £18 per hour for recordings of sufficient quality (and only if full consent and metadata information provided). Crowdsourcing methods were also used when building some other Welsh-language corpora, e.g. *Paldaruo* (Cooper et al., 2019), Mozilla Common Voice and *Cysill Ar-lein* Corpus (Prys et al., 2016), among others.

It was hypothesised that a volunteering-based approach to crowdsourcing would be particularly powerful in the Welsh-language context. This hypothesis was based on the notion that there is community pride and an interest in sustaining and 'growing' the language (evidenced partly by the high levels of contributor engagement seen in the development of the e-language pilot, Chapter 2). To facilitate this approach, the project team developed a bespoke bilingual data collection app, available via iOS, Android and through a web-based interface (an advertisement for this, widely distributed to the Welsh-speaking community, is included in Appendix 3—also see Knight et al., 2021: 46–48 for further discussions of the importance of the 'crowd' in corpus projects). Those who were willing to contribute data via the app were asked to download it and create a user account/profile before giving consent for their conversations to be used and provide their participant and contextual metadata. The participant was then required to record their contribution which was then uploaded to the CorCenCC server. These recordings were downloaded and transcribed by the project team. Reflections on the practicalities and utility of this approach are provided in Chapter 5.

METADATA

In addition to the raw language data collected (i.e. the 'text'), fully documented metadata records (i.e. data about data) are commonly provided in linguistic corpora. This section provides a response to question five:

> 5. What forms of metadata exist and how can this information be obtained from participants/contributors to a corpus?

Metadata 'contains information about the content, source, quality and other characteristics of a particular text' (Adolphs, 2006: 25) and is typically included in a separate document or in the 'header' at the start of each text, and encoded through mark-up language. Metadata plays a key role in organising the ways in which elements of a language are investigated from both a linguistic and social perspective (via search and query tools): 'without metadata, the investigator has nothing but disconnected words of unknowable provenance or authenticity' (Burnard, 2005: 31). This is true regardless of the approach(es) used to underpin how a corpus is designed and built.

Love et al. provide a useful distinction between the different 'types' of metadata in corpora: 'at the level of the text (i.e., situational variables representing features of the recording as a whole) and at the sub-text level (i.e., social variables at the level of the speaker)' (Love et al., 2019: 300). These levels are further divided into more specific groupings, with, for example, 'categorical' (i.e. non-continuous and fixed/defined in terms of the information that can be provided—e.g. date) and 'non-categorical' (i.e. continuous, with wider scope for variation—e.g. conversation length) types of metadata as forms of text-level descriptors, including (adapted from Love et al., 2019: 303):

- Categorical: year of recording, recording period, number of speakers, transcription conventions, sample release information, transcriber.
- Non-categorical (situational): recording length and date, speaker ID, location of recording, inter-speaker relationship (e.g. family members), topics covered, activity description (what participants

were doing while recording the conversation), selected characteristics of conversation type.

The former set is somewhat easier to define and plan for in advance of data collection. The specific format and nature of these descriptors, and the weight and prominence of these, naturally differ from one corpus to the next, depending on its individual aims and purpose.

To collect metadata from contributors to a corpus, decisions need to be made regarding what information will be gathered from them (typically via a metadata form). The 2011 census (ONS, 2011) gave a useful indication of the demography of Welsh speakers in Wales and provided a helpful guideline for developing the speaker/author information (i.e. metadata) forms for the CorCenCC project. The Welsh Language Use Survey (Welsh Government, 2014) was also drawn upon, to inform our knowledge of contributor's Welsh-language acquisition and use. All contributors to the corpus were requested to complete the forms, with an emphasis on individuals providing spoken data in particular.

To provide the most benefit for researching the relationship between demographic categories and language use, full and detailed metadata information is required with, ideally, concrete information provided (i.e. rather than contributors repeatedly abstaining from providing responses to items, etc.). In practice, however, this is not always possible. Participants/contributors are within their rights to not provide detailed personal information if they desire not to: they should not (and cannot) be forced to do so.

The broad metadata categories in CorCenCC's speaker/author information form (Appendix 4) are:

- name (for record creation only, not published/released)
- year of birth
- gender
- place of residence
- occupation
- local dialect area/area that has most influenced the way contributors speak
- Welsh-language ability.

The four items after *name* will be briefly explained below, before a more detailed discussion around the questions of dialect influence and Welsh-language ability is presented. Chapter 5 reports on the number of responses to questions relating to each item that were received from contributors of spoken, written and e-language data, respectively.

Year of birth/gender: By cross-referencing the participant's year of birth with the date of the recording, an approximate age for them at the time of recording could be calculated. Regarding gender, CorCenCC's speaker/author information forms included the options of 'Male', 'Female', 'Other' and 'Prefer not to say'.

Place of residence: A question asked of both BNC 1994 and the *Paldaruo* corpus of Welsh (Cooper et al., 2019) contributors, for example, was where they currently live. In the case of the BNC 1994, this is expressed in terms of country and town, whereas contributors to *Paldaruo* were asked for region of residence. CorCenCC's speaker/author information form's question 'where do you live' provides a closed set of possible responses comprising the 22 local authorities in Wales (see Table 5.6 for full list).

Occupation: The speaker/author information forms included a tick-box question relating to current employment status, with the following options:

- full-time student
- never worked/long-term unemployed
- employed/retired/short-term unemployed.

This was coupled with a free-text space for contributors who indicated that they were employed/retired/short-term unemployed to detail their current or previous role. Based on the free-text description, specific occupations were then categorised using the online National Statistics Socio-economic Classification system tagging tool (NS-SEC, ONS, n.d.), when uploaded to CorCenCC's Data Management Tool (see Chapter 4). NS-SEC categories combine a person's occupation title with information about their employment status, whether they are employed or self-employed, and whether they supervise other employees. These categorisation tools provide labels at various levels of granularity. A decision was made to categorise contributors according to 'major group' occupations (and not their detailed 'analytic' class), using the Standard Occupation Coding scheme (SOC2010—ONS, 2010), as follows:

1. Managers, directors and senior officials
2. Professional occupations
3. Associate professional and technical occupations
4. Administrative and secretarial occupations
5. Skilled trades occupations
6. Caring, leisure and other service occupations
7. Sales and customer service occupations
8. Process, plant and machine operatives
9. Elementary occupations.

NS-SEC categories were used for, for example, the collection of metadata in the Spoken BNC2014 and are recognised as a government standard. As these categories are valid in the Welsh-language context, they were deemed appropriate for use in CorCenCC.

Local dialect area: When demographic metadata is collected for national corpora (including the original BNC 1994), participants are sometimes asked for their nationality and birthplace. In a Welsh-language context, however, it is often more helpful to ask for participants' region of upbringing, since this is likely to be more indicative of their linguistic background than how they choose to define their nationality and/or where they were born. The project team embarked on extensive deliberations regarding how many Welsh dialects there are, how to differentiate between them and how best to represent them in questions in the speaker/author information form. It was necessary to consider potential users of CorCenCC and what search queries they might make within the corpus. For example, those interested in Welsh dialectology might want to examine whether there is any evidence of traditional Welsh dialects (e.g. *Gwenhwyseg*—the historical dialect of south-east Wales) in contemporary Welsh. For such users, the collection of metadata according to historical dialect boundaries may have been useful. However, historically important geographical obstacles such as mountains and rivers that in the past have contributed to dialectal variation are no longer as important, given the population's increased mobility and the influence of the media (Thomas and Thomas, 1989: 9). It was decided, then, that these historical distinctions were not fit-for-purpose.

Another potential user group is learners and teachers of Welsh who may desire to filter corpus data according to the dialect they are learning/teaching. To these users it might have made sense to use generalised dialect areas, e.g. north/south-west/south-east. However, there is no single answer to how dialects of Welsh should be categorised for pedagogical purposes. Anecdotally, schoolteachers appear to allude mainly to a north–south division. Traditionally, in the field of Welsh for Adults, for example, materials have been divided into north and south Wales Welsh, but a 2012 report on future Welsh for Adults materials suggested a three-way divide: north, south-west and south-east (Mac Giolla Chríost et al., 2012: 205). Even offering three choices of dialects is problematic: as well as catering for target users such as those in education, CorCenCC needed to ensure that the dialect choices offered would be appropriate to the corpus contributors themselves.

An alternative approach was used in the *Paldaruo* project, with contributors asked to label their own Welsh as one of five varieties, based on five options they also used for questions posed about regions of upbringing and residence (while noting that their accent might differ from their actual location): 'Choose the area that your accent comes from (even if you live somewhere else)'. This five-way division seemed sensible to replicate. Also, although there are no official statistics as to how many speakers of each dialect there are, by using the same categories as *Paldaruo*, there was at least the possibility of comparing CorCenCC with *Paldaruo*. The distribution of speakers across the five categories in *Paldaruo* follows (Canolfan Bedwyr, n.d.).

- *De ddwyrain Cymru*/south-east Wales: 14.12%
- *De orllewin Cymru*/south-west Wales: 18.29%
- *Gogledd ddwyrain Cymru*/north-east Wales: 10.42%
- *Gogledd orllewin Cymru*/north-west Wales: 42.82%
- *Canolbarth Cymru*/mid-Wales: 14.3%

These percentages might, however, not be reliable indicators of the dialects of the entire Welsh-speaking population. Of the *Paldaruo* project participants resident in Wales, 38.87% were living in north-west Wales (Canolfan Bedwyr, n.d.) and over 82% of them had a north-west Wales accent. However, according to the 2011 census (ONS, 2011), only 26.01% of Welsh speakers live in north-west Wales (counting speakers from Anglesey, Gwynedd and Conwy). It is likely, then, that the *Paldaruo* dialect percentages are slightly skewed towards north-west Wales. Despite this slight skew, the question 'which regions of Wales have most influenced the way you speak Welsh?' was deemed appropriate to include in CorCenCC's speaker/author contribution form. Note that the plural form was used for this question (while *Paldaruo* used the singular). This was to encourage contributors to cite more than one region, if relevant, although they were not restricted to this: a single region would, of course, be a valid response.

Other potentially useful metadata includes how often contributors speak Welsh and in which contexts. For example, those who regularly use Welsh in the workplace arguably use the language differently from those who never use it for work purposes. Also, for CorCenCC, a question about the proportion of a participant's communication that happens in Welsh was included. The response to this question includes a set of 4 closed (tick-box) categories: up to 24%, 25–49%, 50–74% and 75%+.

Welsh-language ability: This brings the discussion to matters of how to differentiate between learners and 'fluent' or 'confident' speakers of Welsh. This distinction is not necessarily as straightforward as, for example, asking participants to note whether Welsh was their first (L1) or second (L2) language. There are many paths to becoming a proficient user of Welsh. Asking about a participant's 'mother tongue' is not necessarily relevant in the Welsh-language context, where a number of Welsh speakers grow up bilingually whether their parents speak Welsh or not, thanks to Welsh-medium education, for example. It is not uncommon to have a 'complicated personal linguistic history' with the Welsh language (Fitzpatrick, 2009: 46). Fitzpatrick discusses a participant in her own study who 'identified Welsh as his first language' but had subsequently 'operated in English from when he was three years old'. This speaker had then gone on to relearn Welsh after retiring.

Participants were asked to respond to a series of questions that could, collectively, provide some insight into their Welsh-language ability. First, categories adapted from responses to the Welsh Language Use Survey (Welsh Government, 2014: 2) question 'where did you develop your Welsh language skills?' were used, as this could provide a basis for classifying participants as either L1 or L2 users of Welsh. For example, a participant who ticked that they had attended 'Welsh-medium/bilingual education' can be classified as L1 (regardless of the language used at home), whereas an L2 user or 'learner' might be one who acquired the language either through 'English-medium school' or on a 'Welsh for adults' course', for example.

The exact point at which an L2 learner becomes an L1 speaker of Welsh is not easy to define. To account for this, participants were also asked to self-define their status as a 'learner' and to self-rate their language proficiency. The Welsh Language Use Survey (National Survey Team, 2015: 2) offers a choice of four descriptions of language ability: 'I'm fluent in Welsh', 'I can speak a fair amount of Welsh', 'I can speak only a little Welsh' and 'I can just say a few words'. In a similar vein, Fitzpatrick offers six descriptions (based on IELTS band descriptors—Fitzpatrick, 2009: 45):

1. **Limited**: My basic competence is limited to familiar situations; I have frequent problems in understanding and expression; I am not able to use complex language.
2. **Modest**: I have partial command of the language, coping with overall meaning in most situations, though am likely to make many mistakes; I should be able to handle basic communication in my own field.
3. **Competent**: I have generally effective command of the language, despite some inaccuracies, inappropriacies and misunderstandings; I can use and understand fairly complex language, particularly in familiar situations.
4. **Good**: I have operational command of the language, though with occasional inaccuracies, inappropriacies and misunderstandings in some situations; generally, I handle complex language well and understand detailed reasoning.
5. **Very good**: I have fully operational command of the language with only occasional unsystematic inaccuracies and inappropriacies; misunderstandings may occur in unfamiliar situations; I handle complex detailed argumentation well.
6. **Expert**: I have fully operational command of the language; appropriate, accurate and fluent with complete understanding.

As these descriptions are very detailed, the expectation was that they would offer sufficient scope for speakers to identify a category that best described them. For CorCenCC's speaker/author information form, the descriptions were shortened to the following options, to ease their processing by the participants:

Welsh-Language ability:

- I can use and understand everyday expressions and basic introductions
- I can communicate basic information in everyday situations
- I can communicate about familiar topics
- I can communicate about a wide range of topics
- I can communicate fluently in almost all situations.

The six options proposed by Fitzpatrick were reduced to five here, with the amalgamation of 'modest' and 'competent' to represent the response of 'I can communicate basic information in everyday situations'. An additional, self-identification question was added: 'would you describe yourself as a learner of Welsh?', coupled with another open response question: 'if you have ticked "Yes", please state the level of your most recent Welsh course'.

Other metadata categories often included in spoken corpora relate to the recordings themselves, not merely the participants: LER-BIML (Wilson, 2002; Wilson et al., 2002) and the Patagonia corpus (Deuchar, 2012), for example, note the location/setting of the speech events, e.g. in the home. For CorCenCC, this information was also, as far as possible, manually noted by the researcher and/or self-defined by the speaker/author. For recordings made via the app, contributors were instead asked to provide additional contextual information after a recording had taken place and was saved to the app. This information included the context and genre(s) of the recording (from a pre-defined list), who was involved in the conversation, and any additional relevant information.

Also regarded as useful metadata for corpora is the audience of a spoken text—including both the participants and others within earshot (see Crowdy, 1993: 264)—and the participants' relationship to one another (Crowdy, 1993: 265; Wilson, 2002; Wilson et al., 2002). For more formal genres such as speeches or TV and radio programmes, details as to whether a text was scripted before being spoken, and whether it had been translated from another language were also useful. These forms of metadata were, where possible, also collected for CorCenCC, as part of the 'additional' information pertaining to individual recordings in the app, or via fieldnotes where recordings were manually collected by the project researchers.

Demographic Targets: Spoken

It is important to underline here that while the components of the design frames seen in Chapter 2 were based principally on contexts and genres, speaker/contributor demographics should also be considered in the planning phase of building a corpus, so that the language data collected represents the speakers themselves, not only their production and reception of the language.

In the context of CorCenCC, the aim was to include speakers/contributors from a representative range of ages, occupations and genders located in different geographical regions of Wales, across different language varieties (regional and social). There was also a desire for the corpus to reflect the proportion of 'Learners or New Speakers of Welsh' among the Welsh-speaking population. A consideration of the demographic categories, and the establishment of broad targets within them was also carried out in relation to CorCenCC's spoken sub-corpus design specifically, once the specific metadata categories had been established. While demographic profiles did not serve as rigid 'targets', they served as a helpful outline of the sort of data that was desirable to include, as they provided a good representation of what the Welsh-speaking population in Wales might look like.

First, data from the 2011 census (ONS, 2011) provided information on the ages of the Welsh-speaking population:

- 3–19: 14.34%
- 20–29: 16.58%
- 30–39: 13.24%
- 40–49: 14.15%
- 50–59: 12.65%
- 60–69: 12.81%
- 70+: 16.23%

The age group with the highest number of Welsh speakers is 20–29, with fluctuations in numbers across the groups. Second, regarding the gender of contributors, the 2011 census data indicates that there is not a 50:50 split between female and male speakers of Welsh: in fact, of those able to speak Welsh, 53.4% are female and 46.6% are male (ONS, 2011). These distributions provided a useful guide for the ages/genders of contributors to represent when collecting data.

As there was an aim to gather data from participants in different geographical regions of Wales, it was important to consider targeting a representative percentage of Welsh speakers from all the twenty-two unitary authorities in Wales, as detailed in Table 3.1. Aiming to proportionally align the percentage of Welsh speakers listed in each authority, with the amount of data collected from contributors located in each of these regions was a useful target for CorCenCC.

In terms of Welsh-language proficiency, the Welsh Language Use survey indicated that 47% of Welsh speakers are fluent; 21% can speak a fair amount; 23% can only speak a little Welsh while 8% can just say a few words (National Survey Team, 2015). Aiming for an approximate alignment to this would provide a dataset that, arguably, represents the range of proficiencies of Welsh speakers.

Finally, in terms of occupation, the census indicates that for Welsh speakers aged 16+, around 12% are full-time students, circa 4% are long-term unemployed and circa 84% are either retired or employed

Table 3.1 Welsh speakers in each of local authorities in Wales (ONS, 2011)

Local authority	Welsh speakers	% of Wales total	Local authority	Welsh speakers	% of Wales total
Isle of Anglesey	38,568	6.86%	Merthyr Tydfil	5028	0.89%
Blaenau Gwent	5284	0.94%	Monmouthshire	8780	1.56%
Bridgend	13,103	2.33%	Neath Port Talbot	20,698	3.68%
Caerphilly	19,251	3.43%	Newport	13,002	2.31%
Cardiff	36,735	6.54%	Pembrokeshire	22,786	4.05%
Carmarthenshire	78,048	13.89%	Powys	23,990	4.27%
Ceredigion	34,964	6.22%	Rhondda Cynon Taf	27,779	4.94%
Conwy	30,600	5.44%	Swansea	26,332	4.69%
Denbighshire	22,236	3.96%	Torfaen	8641	1.54%
Flintshire	19,343	3.44%	Vale of Glamorgan	13,189	2.35%
Gwynedd	77,000	13.70%	Wrexham	16,659	2.96%

(ONS, 2011). The following results also provide useful information on occupations of the employed/retired to represent (ONS, 2011):

1. Managers, directors and senior officials: 17,281 speakers
2. Professional occupations: 45,212 speakers
3. Associate professional and technical occupations: 24,188 speakers
4. Administrative and secretarial occupations: 23,711 speakers
5. Skilled trades occupations: 35,109 speakers
6. Caring, leisure and other service occupations: 27,191 speakers
7. Sales and customer service occupations: 18,092 speakers
8. Process, plant and machine operatives: 13,892 speakers
9. Elementary occupations: 23,085 speakers.

Combined, the census and occupation figures give a good indication of the employment/unemployment/student status of Welsh speakers. The aim was, therefore, to sample data along these lines:

- Full-time students = 11.9%
- Never worked/Long-term unemployed = 4.0%
- Occupation 1: Managers, directors and senior officials—7.6% of 84.1% = 6.4%
- Occupation 2: Professional occupations—19.9% of 84.1% = 16.7%
- Occupation 3: Associate professional and technical occupations—10.6% of 84.1% = 8.9%
- Occupation 4: Administrative and secretarial occupations—10.4% of 84.1% = 8.8%
- Occupation 5: Skilled trades occupations—15.4% of 84.1% = 13.0%
- Occupation 6: Caring, leisure and other service occupations—11.9% of 84.1% = 10.0%
- Occupation 7: Sales and customer service occupations—7.9% of 84.1% = 6.7%
- Occupation 8: Process, plant and machine operatives—6.1% of 84.1% = 5.1%
- Occupation 9: Elementary occupations—10.1% of 84.1% = 8.5%

Regarding written data in CorCenCC, while there was an aim to record full metadata information concerning the authors' linguistic backgrounds, etc., (using the speaker/author information forms as discussed above), this proved to be difficult to account for. This information was often difficult to trace (e.g. if there were multiple authors of a text) or simply was not made available to the team. For this reason, it was decided not to set specific targets regarding the location and other demographic categories of contributors in this data mode.

This difficulty was also faced when collecting e-language metadata. While, again, speaker/author information forms were used, in many instances contributors simply offered their written consent in the body of an email or signed the consent form without completing the additional demographic information. Consequently, although a wide cross-section of individuals was encouraged to contribute data to the corpus, no specific targets relating to contributor profiles were created for e-language either.

COPYRIGHT, PERMISSIONS AND ETHICS

A detailed consideration of copyright, permission and ethics is vital at every stage of the corpus design and building process. This is of particular importance if, as with CorCenCC, the corpus is to be made openly available and accessible (CorCenCC and its associated tools are made available under programme and data licences GPL v3.0 and CC-BY-SA). The remaining sections of this chapter respond to question six:

6. What are some of the key ethical issues and challenges that should be considered before collecting data for a corpus?

Within a UK context, it is important that the processes involved in the production, analysis, publication and sharing of data are compliant with the requirements of the General Data Protection Regulations (GDPR, see Tikkinen-Piri et al., 2017—note that these requirements may change in the UK context as a consequence of Brexit). The typical practice in addressing ethics at a professional or institutional level is for corpus developers to ensure that formal written consent is received from all participants prior to recording or collecting data. Conventionally, this consent stipulates how recordings are to take place and/or how the data is harvested, how much data is sampled, how data is (re)presented and outlines the research purposes for which it is used. While, for example, a participant's *consent to record* may be relatively easy to obtain, and commonly involves a signature on a consent form, it is also important to consider *consent to distribute* recorded material, that is, how the recorded data is to be stored, accessed and/or distributed and by whom. In the case of CorCenCC, it was vital that all contributors were aware that the corpus would be released under an open licence to academic researchers, community users of Welsh and the wider language technology community.

Although, in alignment with common practice in applied linguistics research (see the British Association for Applied Linguistics 'Recommendations on Good Practice in Applied Linguistics', BAAL, 2021), participants have the right to withdraw their consent at any stage of the research process, they need to be told that once the corpus is published and/or distributed, it is impossible to deal with requests for data retraction or redaction of consent at that stage.

In the development of many national corpora, particularly those in major languages such as English, a pragmatic approach to permission is often used. The written BNC 2014, for example, operated on the understanding that 'it seems that for legal and practical reasons permission will not have to be sought to include things which are posted publicly online in the written BNC 2014' (Hawtin, 2018: 209), and to use up to 5% of written texts, given that this amount falls within the prescriptions of 'fair dealing'. However, for more ethical (rather than simply legal and practical) reasons, it was conceded that it might be beneficial for the CorCenCC team to collect permissions even where these principles apply. Given that the Welsh-language community is relatively small, there is a higher chance of individuals being recognised by dialect or a local connection between speakers/contributors than in a language community with many millions of speakers. The approaches to permission and anonymity needed to be implemented with sensitivity to ensure as much anonymity for members of this community as possible.

When building CorCenCC, consent forms were drawn up by the project team in consultation with the legal unit at the lead institution, Cardiff University, before the data collection phase. These consent forms, which included forms (all bilingual), for the individuals listed below, were approved for use by all project partner institutions:

A. Individuals
B. Children
C. Parents
D. Young people
E. Businesses
F. Educational institutions

Separate legal agreements/contracts were entered into with project stakeholders and major contributors.

Consent forms were distributed directly to participants by the project researchers at the point when they were recruited. For example, for potential e-language and written language contributors, consent forms were sent via email during recruitment, while spoken language contributors received a hard copy to sign, or were asked to give consent via the app, before making recordings. The project researchers took responsibility in ensuring that consent was obtained prior to data collection. This approach differs slightly from that used for the Spoken BNC 2014, whereby, through the adoption of the PPSR approach (Shirk et al., 2012), 'contributors took responsibility for making recordings and for gathering consent and metadata from all speakers they recorded' (Love et al., 2017: 328). Again, our more rigid approach was used in recognition of the size and dynamics of the language community, and to ensure all contributors were fully complicit and ethically protected in the use of their data.

A further issue when considering ethical approaches to corpus is the notion of anonymity. Anonymity functions to protect the identities of those who are involved, or mentioned, in an interaction or passage of text. To achieve this, the names of participants and third parties, along with personal information/identifiers such as addresses, phones numbers, email addresses and so on, are often 'de-identified' (using pseudonyms or other anonymisation tags—see McEnery et al., 2017), or completely omitted in the corpus text. This process of de-identification can be made at the transcription stage, or as a subsequent step.

Variations of the following statement were included in all consent forms:

> Written data and transcribed spoken data may be included in the corpus or used in published works or academic presentations or for other academic purposes. Cardiff University will try to ensure that all such data will be anonymised to such an extent that the identity of the author/speaker and

references to individual people and personal information should not be retrievable, but will not have any legal responsibility if any personal data which has been anonymised is re-identified by any means.

If you wish to opt out of our anonymisation procedures so that your name appears in the corpus, please tick the box marked 'I wish to opt out of text anonymisation'.

N.B. Even when this option is selected, the CorCenCC team will continue to anonymise the text to try to ensure that people who you discuss in your written data, digital language data, and spoken data remain anonymous.

This statement underlines that the team will 'try to ensure' anonymity in the data, focusing primarily on the de-identification of 'references to individual people and personal information'. It can be a challenge to achieve full anonymity in data records and, as stated in BAAL's 'recommendations on Good Practice in Applied Linguistics' (BAAL, 2021: 6):

In some cases, such as participatory or collaborative research and some forms of internet research, anonymity may be impossible or unfavourable, as where an internet site's regulations state that data should not be altered, or where an author, or joint practitioner/researcher, wishes to be acknowledged. In such cases, specific regulatory frameworks governing research sites, and/or the autonomy of individual informants, must be negotiated.

The level of anonymity required for a specific type of contribution and/or from a specific contributor is something that is negotiated on a case-by-case basis as there is no universal best practice for this process. If data is freely available and sourced from the public domain, no alterations to the text are usually required.

The final question is an important consideration here:

7. When and why might it be appropriate to modify/change corpus data?

Typically, corpora are not edited or modified in any way as there is an emphasis on data being as authentic as possible. Any form of editing and/or modification of data is effectively seen to 'distort' the language and is at odds with the main advantage of using a corpus approach: exploring language as it is *actually* used. Exceptions to this rule do, however, exist. This is typically in the case of potentially sensitive and/or controversial or divisive language and opinions (see McEnery & Hardie, 2012). The developers of CorCenCC did not foresee the collection of many examples falling into this category. However, the potential for some texts to include content of a sensitive or explicit nature could not be discounted. Clearly this was a consideration in the creation of a resource designed for use by those in school under 18 years of age.

Focus groups and questionnaires with teachers and educators flagged concerns about the appropriateness of using CorCenCC in a classroom context if 'inappropriate' language was to be included. To mitigate these concerns, the CorCenCC team made the strategic decision to create two different ways into the corpus: the conventional corpus query tool interface and the distinct pedagogic toolkit, *Y Tiwtiadur* (see Chapter 4). While *Y Tiwtiadur* draws on evidence from the complete CorCenCC dataset, examples in this tool are taken from texts that are tagged as being 'suitable' for a young audience. A similar need was identified by the developers of the SCOTS corpus (Anderson et al., 2007), as this was designed as a public resource for all ages and types of users. Where appropriate, data in SCOTS was marked up with the following content labels (Anderson et al., 2007):

> Lesser—this document contains language which some may find offensive
> Serious—this document contains strong or offensive language.

However, the SCOTS corpus query tools do not have provisions for filtering out results from the documents when performing searches, they simply identify texts that have been tagged as offensive (and to what extent) in the results (so they can be avoided, if required). The workflows used to tag texts in terms of their 'suitability' and to anonymise data in CorCenCC are discussed in the next chapter.

Once data has been ethically collected, in line with the recommendations and approaches outlined in this chapter, the next phases of corpus building process are the processing and (re)presenting of corpus data. These phases will be discussed in Chapter 4.

REFERENCES

Adda, G., Mariani, J., Besacier, L., & Gelas, H. (2014). *Crowdsourcing for speech: Economic, legal and ethical analysis*. Retrieved from https://hal.archives-ouvertes.fr/hal-01067110 [Accessed 20/06/2021].

Adolphs, S. (2006). *Introducing electronic text analysis*. Cambridge University Press.

Anderson, J., Beavan, D., & Kay, C. (2007). SCOTS: Scottish corpus of texts and speech. In J. Beal, K. Corrigan, & H. Moisl (Eds.), *Creating and digitizing language corpora: Volume 1—Synchronic databases* (pp. 17–34). Palgrave Macmillan.

Anthony, L. (2017). *AntFileConverter (Version 1.2.1)* [Software]. Waseda University. Retrieved from https://www.laurenceanthony.net/software [Accessed 20/06/2021].

Asheghi, N., Sharoff, S., & Markert, K. (2014). Designing and evaluating a reliable corpus of web genres via crowd-sourcing. In *Proceedings of the Language Resources and Evaluation Conference* (pp. 1339–1346). Reykjavik, Iceland.

BAAL. (2021). *Recommendations on good practice in applied linguistics*. Retrieved from http://www.baal.org.uk [Accessed 20/06/2021].

Boleda, G., Bott, S., Meza, R., Castillo, C., Badia, T., & López, V. (2006). CUCWeb: A Catalan corpus built from the Web. In *Proceedings of the WAC'06 (2nd International Workshop on Web as Corpus)* (pp. 19–26). Bielefeld University, Bielefeld.

Burnard, L. (2005). Developing linguistic corpora: Metadata for corpus work. In M. Wynne (Ed.), *Developing linguistic corpora: A guide to good practice* (pp. 30–46). Oxbow Books.

Caines, A., Bentz, C., Graham, C., Polzehl, T., & Buttery, P. (2016). Crowdsourcing a multilingual speech corpus: Recording, transcription and annotation of the CROWDED CORPUS. In *Proceedings of the Language Resources and Evaluation (LREC)*(pp. 2145–2152). Portorož, Slovenia.

Canolfan Bedwyr. (n.d.). *Metadata questions: Paldaruo app*. Language Technologies Unit. Retrieved from http://techiaith.bangor.ac.uk/paldaruo/metadata-questions/?lang=en [Accessed 20/06/2021].

Clematide, S., Furrer, L., & Volk, M. (2016). Crowdsourcing an OCR gold standard for a German and French heritage corpus. In *Proceedings of the Language Resources and Evaluation (LREC)* (pp. 975–982). Portorož, Slovenia.

Cooper, S., Jones, D. B., & Prys, D. (2019). Crowdsourcing the Paldaruo speech corpus of Welsh for speech technology. *Information, 10*(8), 247–258.

Crowdy, S. (1993). Spoken corpus design. *Literary and Linguistic Computing, 8*, 259–265.

Deuchar, M. (2012). *The Bangor Patagonia corpus* [Online]. Bangor University. Retrieved from http://www.bangortalk.org.uk/speakers.php?c=patagonia [Accessed 20/06/2021].

3 (META)DATA COLLECTION 101

Deuchar, M., Webb-Davies, P., & Donnelly, K. (2018). *Building and using the Siarad corpus*. John Benjamins.

Fitzpatrick, T. (2009). Word association profiles in a first and second language: Puzzles and problems. In T. Fitzpatrick & A. Barfield (Eds.), *Lexical processing in second language learners* (pp. 38–52). Multilingual Matters.

Gries, S. T., & Newman, J. (2014). Creating and using corpora. In D. Sharma & R. J. Podesva (Eds.), *Research methods in linguistics* (pp. 257–287). Cambridge University Press.

Gruenstein, A., McGraw, I., & Sutherland, A. (2009). A self-transcribing speech corpus: Collecting continuous speech with an online educational game. In *Proceedings of the ISCA International Workshop on Speech and Language Technology in Education (SLaTE 2009)* (pp. 109–112). Warwickshire, England.

Hawtin, A. (2018). *The written British national corpus 2014: Design, compilation and analysis*. Unpublished PhD thesis, Lancaster University.

Howe, J. (2006). *The Rise of Crowdsourcing. Wired Magazine, 14*, 1–4.

Knight, D., Morris, S., & Fitzpatrick, T. (2021). *Corpus design and construction in minoritised language contexts: The national corpus of contemporary Welsh*. Palgrave.

Love, R., Brezina, V., McEnery, A., Hawtin, A., Hardie, A., & Dembry, C. (2019). Functional variation in the spoken BNC 2014 and the potential for register analysis. *Register Studies, 1*(2), 296–317.

Love, R., Dembry, C., Hardie, A., Brezina, V., & McEnery, T. (2017). The spoken BNC 2014: Designing and building a spoken corpus of everyday conversations. *International Journal of Corpus Linguistics, 22*, 319–344.

Mac Giolla Chríost, D., Carlin, P., Davies, S., Fitzpatrick, T., Jones, A. P., Heath-Davies, R., Marshall, J., Morris, S., Price, A., Vanderplank, R., Walter, C., & Wray, A. (2012). *Adnoddau, dulliau ac ymagweddau dysgu ac addysgu ym maes Cymraeg i Oedolion: astudiaeth ymchwil gynhwysfawr ac adolygiad beirniadol o'r ffordd ymlaen* [Welsh for adults teaching and learning approaches, methodologies and resources: A comprehensive research study and critical review of the way forward]. Welsh Government. Retrieved from https://llyw.cymru/sites/default/files/statistics-and-research/2019-08/130424-welsh-adults-teaching-learning-approaches-cy.pdf [Accessed 20/06/2021].

McEnery, A., & Hardie, A. (2012). *Corpus linguistics: Method, theory and practice* [Companion Website]. Cambridge University Press. Retrieved from: http://corpora.lancs.ac.uk/clmtp/answers.php?chapter=3&type=questions [Accessed 20/06/2021].

McEnery, T., Love, R., & Brezina, V. (2017). Compiling and analysing the spoken British national corpus 2014. *International Journal of Corpus Linguistics, 22*(3), 311–318.

McGraw, I., Gruenstein, A., & Sutherland, A. (2009). A self-labeling speech corpus: Collecting spoken words with an online educational game. *Proceedings of the INTERSPEECH 2009—10th Annual Conference of the International Speech Communication Association* (pp. 3031–3034). Brighton, United Kingdom.

National Survey Team, W. G. (2015). *Welsh language use survey 2013-15: Welsh language ability.* Retrieved from https://gov.wales/welsh-language-use-survey-2013-2015 [Accessed 20/06/2021].

ONS (Office for National Statistics). (2010). *SOC2010 volume 1: Structure and descriptions of unit groups.* Retrieved from https://www.ons.gov.uk/methodology/classificationsandstandards/standardoccupationalclassificationsoc/soc2010/soc2010volume1structureanddescriptionsofunitgroups#summarising-changes-to-the-classification-structure-introduced-in-soc2010 [Accessed 20/06/2021].

ONS (Office for National Statistics). (2011). *Census: Digitised boundary data (England and Wales)* [Computer File]. Retrieved from https://borders.ukdataservice.ac.uk/ [Accessed 20/06/2021].

ONS (Office for National Statistics). (n.d.). *ONS occupation coding tool* [Online]. Retrieved from https://onsdigital.github.io/dp-classification-tools/standard-occupational-classification/ONS_SOC_occupation_coding_tool.html [Accessed 20/06/2021].

Prys, D., Prys, G., & Jones, D. (2016). Cysill Ar-lein: A corpus of written contemporary Welsh compiled from an online spelling and grammar checker. In *Proceedings of the Tenth International Conference on Language Resources and Evaluation (LREC '16)* (pp. 3261–3264). Portorož, Slovenia.

Sabou, M., Bontcheva, K., Derczynski, L., & Scharl, A. (2014). Corpus Annotation through Crowdsourcing: Towards Best Practice Guidelines. *Proceedings of the 9th International Conference on Language Resources and Evaluation (LREC'14)* (pp. 859–866). Portoroz, Slovenia.

Scannell, K. (2007). The Crúbadán project: Corpus building for under-resourced languages. *Cahiers Du Cental, 5*(1), 1–10.

Shirk, J., Ballard, H., Wilderman, C., Phillips, T., Wiggins, A., Jordan, R., McCallie, E., Minarchek, M., Lewenstein, B., Krasny, M., & Bonney, R. (2012). Public participation in scientific research: A framework for deliberate design. *Ecology and Society, 17*, 29–48.

Thomas, B., & Thomas, P. W. (1989). *Cymraeg, Cymrâg, Cymrêg: Cyflwyno'r tafodieithoedd* [Welsh: Introducing the dialects]. Gwasg Taf.

Tikkinen-Piri, C., Rohunen, A., & Markkula, J. (2017). EU general data protection regulation: Changes and implications for personal data collecting companies. *Computer Law and Security Review, 34*(1), 134–153.

Welsh Government. (2014). *National survey for Wales—Welsh language use survey 2014–15* [Online]. Retrieved from https://gov.wales/sites/default/

files/statistics-and-research/2018-12/160301-welsh-language-use-in-wales-2013-15-en.pdf [Accessed 20/06/2021].

Wilson, A. (2002). *The language engineering resources for the indigenous minority languages of the British Isles and Ireland project* [Online]. Retrieved from http://www.ling.lancs.ac.uk/biml/ [Accessed 20/06/2021].

Wilson, A., Worth, C., Donnelly, K., Färber, B., Jones, G., Kirk, J., Mills, J., & Prys, D. (2002). *LER-BIML: The corpus: Welsh corpus* [Online]. Lancaster University. Retrieved from: http://www.lancaster.ac.uk/fass/projects/biml/bimls3corpus.htm [Accessed 20/06/2021].

CHAPTER 4

Processing and (Re)presenting Corpora

Abstract Moving on to the final key stages of building a corpus, this chapter provides a brief exploration of approaches to processing and (re)presenting language data for future analysis. The chapter first details the importance of the transcription phase in spoken corpus development and documents how bespoke transcription conventions can be developed for, and employed in, a given target language. The tagging and collation of corpus data (via corpus managers) are also briefly explored, before some exemplar corpus querying tools and CorCenCC's novel pedagogic toolkit, *Y Tiwtiadur*, are presented.

Keywords Transcription · Transcription conventions · Tagging · Corpus managers · Query tools · *Y Tiwtiadur*

OVERVIEW

Once the natural language has been collected, the next stage(s) of building a corpus concerns how the data will be processed and (re)presented for future analysis. This chapter provides a brief insight into how these stages can be approached. Some important generic questions that are answered here are:

© The Author(s), under exclusive license to Springer Nature Switzerland AG 2021
D. Knight et al., *Building a National Corpus*,
https://doi.org/10.1007/978-3-030-81858-6_4

105

> 1. What are the key principles to consider when defining and/or creating transcription conventions?
> 2. How might the anonymisation and suitability checking of corpus data be approached?
> 3. What is the purpose of tagging and what features might be useful to tag in corpora?
> 4. What are corpus managers and what are they used for?
> 5. What are some of the query tools and applications that may be used to facilitate the exploration of corpus data?

Again, while the chapter focuses on CorCenCC as a central case study, the methods and approaches presented here are relevant to building a corpus in any language.

Transcribing Spoken Data

As discussed earlier, at the point of collection, written and e-language data are typically represented in a computer readable text-based format. However, spoken interaction requires an additional stage of processing: transcription. Transcription can involve (Edwards, 1995: 20):

> capturing who said what, in what manner (e.g. prosody, pause, voice quality), to whom, under what circumstances (e.g. setting, activity, participant characteristics and relationships to one another). It includes preservation of various temporal aspects (e.g. pause duration, sequence of events, and simultaneity or overlap of speaker turns or speech and gestures), and some metacomments, or interpretative 'annotations'.

Transcription provides a written record of spoken interaction to enable it to be processed, tagged and analysed in the same way as written and e-language data.

Transcription is a necessarily selective and interpretive process, as a complete and fully precise record of spoken text in written form is near impossible to produce. Nonetheless, a transcription 'is an essential indexing aid to the original' speech (Aston & Burnard, 1997: 42), one that facilitates the research and study of spoken communication in corpora. Originally, there was an intention to include the raw audio recordings in CorCenCC, aligning them with their respective transcriptions (following Talkbank, MacWhinney, 2000), but issues relating to storage capacity, ethics and permissions meant that the published corpus is currently only available in a text-based format.

> 1. What are the key principles to consider when defining and/or creating transcription conventions?

To address this question, this section examines:

   i. Key challenges faced in planning for transcription (including the time and effort needed)
   ii. Considerations for locating or devising your own transcription conventions
   iii. How to operationalise the transcription process, and
   iv. Some approaches to transcriber training and quality control.

Featured in a 'wish-list for future corpora' in 2010 was a hope that 'creating spoken corpora will benefit from technological advances in speech recognition, thus making the task of transcribing spoken language to text files a much more efficient process and more automated task' (Reppen, 2010: 36). Despite the passing of a decade and the ever-increasing sophistication of speech-to-text technologies, a fully accurate automated approach to the transcription of spoken data has still not been developed for languages such as English, so is certainly not available to those working with under-resourced and minoritised languages. Transcription is still 'accomplished by individuals listening to the recordings and transcribing, or keying them, into the computer' (Reppen, 2010: 34). It is a largely manually driven, time consuming, task that persists as 'undeniably the most important bottleneck in corpus compilation' (Schmidt, 2016: 404).

The amount of time taken to transcribe a conversation depends somewhat on the level of detail required in transcription (i.e. the higher the level of detail, the more time consuming and expensive it becomes). Practical considerations such as time and cost are therefore essential to consider when planning the transcription phase. O'Keeffe et al., for example, suggest that it 'takes around two days to transcribe' one hour of audio to the quality required to undertake detailed linguistic analyses (O'Keeffe et al., 2007: 2). In the case of CorCenCC, the level of detail required for the transcription was not equivalent to that required for a necessarily 'detailed linguistic analysis', but was more in line with the approach used in the original BNC 1994, for example, where 'the aim was to transcribe as clearly and economically as possible rather than to represent all the subtleties of the audio recording' (Aston & Burnard, 1997: 36).

The conventions used to transcribe spoken language, again, depend on the aims of the corpus and the questions that it is designed to enable users to answer. While no agreed standards for transcription necessarily exist, shared practices for orthographic transcription are common across more general spoken corpora and/or national corpora with spoken components. The Spoken BNC 1994 and Spoken BNC 2014, for example, use a form of orthographic transcription that enables the quantitative study of usage patterns of 'morphology, lexis, syntax, pragmatics, etc.' (Atkins et al., 1992: 10). This aim is echoed in CorCenCC. The study of phonetics is not directly catered for in the transcription of these corpora, so full phonetic transcription is not provided (although this would be possible in post-hoc, should the audio recordings be made available). This is a similar case for other national corpora, as the bigger and more general the corpus, the broader and more simplified the transcription conventions typically used.

Also common to national (and other spoken) corpora is an emphasis on ensuring that transcriptions represent recorded speech 'as faithfully as possible', achieved by 'transcribing verbatim what the person said regardless of whether it follows the so-called rules of the standard language' (Tagliamonte, 2007: 210). This includes capturing, for example, hesitations, overlaps and false starts, features that represent the 'normal dysfluency' of spoken language (Biber et al., 1999: 1048). Specific conventions/protocols for transcription, including how to capture/represent such 'dysfluency' are important to establish for use when building a spoken corpus.

Despite the lack of agreed 'standards' in transcription, there have been some efforts to align and standardise the encoding of items in a transcript to enhance their readability and reusability (qualities that *all* transcription conventions should strive to adhere to). These include conventions adopted by the Network of European Reference Corpora (NERC), used for the spoken component of the COBUILD project (Sinclair, 1987), and the guidelines for transcribing spoken data recommended by the Text Encoding Initiative (TEI), that were applied to the original BNC 1994 (Sperberg-McQueen & Burnard, 1993). TEI provides a well-defined header structure for documenting transcription information, and a number of tags that offer a method by which certain features of speech can be represented. In the development of the Spoken BNC 2014, the team opted for a modest level of XML (Extensible Markup Language) for use in the corpus rather than the traditional TEI approach (Love et al., 2017a: 339), ensuring that it had a certain level of comparability with TEI and the computer readability of XML. Similarly, the overarching guidelines provided by TEI underpinned some of the decisions made when developing conventions for use in CorCenCC but were modified to include translated versions of tags or elements, facilitating an immersive Welsh-language experience for both transcribers and eventual corpus users.

For an example of transcription conventions used in other Welsh-language corpora, the project team turned to *Siarad* (Deuchar et al., 2018). *Siarad* includes orthographic transcriptions linked directly to the source audio files in the corpus database, with conventions adapted from the CHAT system (MacWhinney, 2000). As the aim of *Siarad* was to facilitate the exploration of the nature of code-switching, variations in pronunciation were not a priority in its development (something also illustrated by the limited variation in the location of the speakers, with three-quarters of the data coming from speakers from the north-west of Wales, Deuchar et al., 2018: 10). Also, the need for consistency in *Siarad* motivated the decision to standardise the Welsh language in the corpus (Deuchar et al., 2018: 159). Both features made *Siarad's* conventions unsuitable for use in CorCenCC, thus bespoke conventions were created.

The aim for CorCenCC was to create written records of spoken data that would reflect the language as it was both used by the participants and heard by the transcribers. There was an aim for CorCenCC's transcription conventions to be as clear and unambiguous, yet as general and user-friendly as possible so they could be re-used by others when transcribing their own recordings. Similar to CANCODE (McCarthy, 1998), the conventions include the use of individual speaker codes such as <S1> and <S2> for each unique contributor and <SG> (male), <SB> (female) or <S?> (unidentified): effectively anonymising all speakers at the first stage of transcription. Guidance for anonymising other features was also provided in the conventions, along with details on how to tag recordings, at the text level, if they contained content deemed inappropriate for young children (discussed below).

Similarly, as with CANCODE, overlapping speech (i.e. across individual speaker turns) is indicated in the conventions by a '+' and where a turn is unfinished or interrupted, or a false start occurs, the tag <-> is utilised. In line with the Spoken BNC 2014, there was an aim to use 'minimal punctuation marks' (Love et al., 2017b: 26) in CorCenCC's transcriptions as speakers often don't speak in 'sentences'. Rather, full stops are utilised to indicate natural breaks and/or extended pauses. This is to allow some of the computational tools to work effectively.

The development of the transcription conventions was an iterative process. An initial version was created and rolled out to a small pool of transcribers for testing. Feedback on the ease of use and transparency of the conventions was received, and any required revisions were made accordingly. For example, transcribers were initially instructed to only use spellings that could also be found in *Geiriadur Prifysgol Cymru* (Dictionary of the Welsh Language). However, when the consistency and quality of the transcriptions were checked, it was discovered that many transcribers were not adhering to these spelling conventions. This had implications for time needed to check and quality control (QC) the transcriptions.

As it turned out, resolving this practical problem aligned with an aim of the project, namely, to capture the rich linguistic diversity of how Welsh is spoken (in terms of accent/dialect). To account for regional variation, the resultant approach used in CorCenCC mirrors that used in the development of the SCOTS corpus, that is, with the use of a form of orthographic transcription that reflects pronunciation as closely as possible (Anderson et al., 2007), rather than suggesting specific conventions and normalised/standardised spellings. In fact, when reporting on the development of SCOTS, in 2007, it was stated that 'at this stage, no Scots spelling conventions have been decided upon, so spellings might have to be normalised at a later date' (Anderson et al., 2007: 25)—and this remains the case.

The various spellings of word were subsequently tagged as instances of a single form, so that searches would be possible without fragmenting the evidence. Guidelines were provided for the level of detail required in broadly transcribing dialectal forms. Specific guidelines were also provided for transcribing non-verbal sounds, numerals and other features. Transcribers were urged to replace omissions with apostrophes and to be consistent with how they did this throughout the transcription. For example, for an omission:

- at the start of the word: *'lly* (*'felly'*), i.e. so, therefore
- in the middle of a word: *lla'th* (*'llaeth'*), i.e. milk
- at the end of a word: *yn yr ha'* (*'yn yr haf'*), i.e. in the summer
- when combining words: (*doe*)*s* + (*y*)*na* + (*ddi*)*m* = *'s'na'm*, i.e. there isn't/aren't

One exception is that no apostrophe was required at the end of plural words such as *geiria* (*geiriau* > words), *petha* (*pethau* > things), *papura* (*papurau* > papers), *'sgidia* (*'sgidiau* > shoes) as this is highly frequent and conventional in written representations of speech already.

When a speaker uses words, phrases or sentences that are in a non-Welsh language (including English), they are enclosed in tags that indicate the language used. The tags <fr> and </fr> , for example, indicate code-switching into French. If the code-switching extends across several speaker turns, the non-Welsh speech is marked for every turn. If it is not possible to identify the language, <*lleferydd di-Gymraeg*> ('non-Welsh speech') is used. In the case of loanwords, i.e. words adopted from one language and incorporated into another, it was decided that there is no need to tag these as instances of code-switching, but instead include them with their Welsh spellings in the transcript. This is because many English words have been incorporated into Welsh and now appear, for example, in *Geiriadur Prifysgol Cymru*.

A range of software tools exists to support the transcription of audio files including: Transana (Woods & Fassnacht, 2007), EXMARaLDA (Wörner & Schmidt, 2009) and ELAN (Wittenburg et al., 2006). It is important to note, however, that not all software may be able to support certain linguistic scripts or characters, so their usability and appropriacy for developing a corpus in a specific language need to be assessed on a case-by-case basis. In terms of the Welsh language, a range of software *is* available to fully support transcription. After initial road-testing of functionalities, Transcriber (https://sourceforge.net/projects/trans/), a freely available software tool for transcribing, segmenting and annotating audio was deemed to be the most accessible and easy-to-use software for this specific context. Transcriber also works with different operating systems and a variety of audio file formats.

The full bilingual transcription conventions and transcriber instructions that were devised for use in CorCenCC are available in the 'documentation' folder on the CorCenCC GitHub site: https://github.com/CorCenCC. The instructions part of this document includes information from how transcribers downloaded and accessed the files from the CorCenCC server, to operating Transcriber, through to the transcribing and anonymising conventions. Three iterations of conventions were produced, each one being refined and updated based on the feedback from the transcribers, on the understanding that transcription guidelines are 'refined as our experience grows' (Anderson et al., 2007: 24).

The workflow for the transcription phase is depicted in Fig. 4.1, with

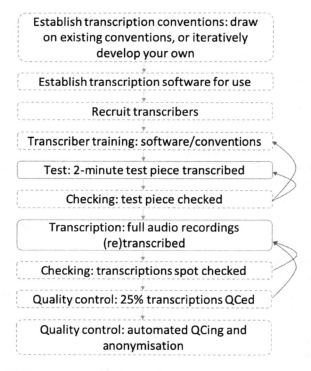

Fig. 4.1 Workflow for transcribing spoken corpora

the stages relevant to the team of transcribers indicated by full lines and those relevant to the research team indicated by dotted lines.

Transcribers were recruited using the same techniques used to recruit participants (Chapter 3), with individuals working for specific transcription companies and institutions also targeted via email, social media and so on (see Appendix 5 for an example of the information sheets used to recruit the transcribers). Once recruited, transcribers were first given extensive training in using the software and conventions and were asked to transcribe a 2-minute test piece. This was checked for accuracy and how well transcribers adhered to the conventions. If the transcriber demonstrated understanding of the conversation, but not the conventions, feedback was provided, and the transcriber was asked to try again. If the transcriber passed the test phase, they were sent full conventions and allocated audio files for transcription. The first transcription returned by a given transcriber was spot-checked for accuracy and understanding, use of transcription conventions, general spelling errors, etc., with checks made to ensure:

- there hadn't been unnecessary standardisation
- non-verbal sounds had been transcribed according to conventions
- where relevant, a full stop, question mark or plus sign (for overlapping speech) was used at the end of lines, but no other punctuation (e.g. commas)
- speaker tags (e.g. <S1> , <S2>) were labelled
- conventions regarding repetition, false starts were accurate
- instances of <D> (guesses) and <aneglur> (unclear sections) were reasonable
- anonymisation had been carried out and the text tagged with <rhegi> (swearing) where applicable
- transcribers were given feedback on any errors found—if major issues were found, transcribers were asked to correct them (revised files were spot-checked again).

A sub-team of quality controllers (QCers) was then recruited from a pool of transcribers who had produced high-quality transcriptions in good time. 25% of the transcriptions were randomly selected and sent to QCers who were tasked with checking/correcting, as appropriate, 1000 words from the transcription (if the transcription was <1000 words, the QCer checked it all). The QCer recorded the number of corrections they made (i.e. <10, 10–50, >50) and whether the sample was taken from the beginning, middle or end of the transcript (to ensure that the QCing—quality controlling—process was varied). If >50 mistakes existed, the transcriber corrected the whole transcription (other work from the transcriber was then also checked), if 10–50 mistakes were found, the team checked the mistakes for severity and revised accordingly. The emphasis on producing high-quality transcriptions was underpinned by the multiple checking stages undertaken.

In an ideal world, 100% of each transcription would be checked and double checked for accuracy, but given the limited time and resources available, this was not possible. It is perhaps never possible to gain complete accuracy in transcription. As a final stage of quality control, automated scripts (i.e. a list of commands that are executed by a computer to automatically perform a task) were also run over the data to ensure that transcription and anonymisation conventions, and formatting, were consistent (discussed below).

AUTOMATED ANONYMISATION AND SUITABILITY TAGGING

Once the written and e-language files had been collected, and the spoken audio recordings transcribed, the next stage of data processing involved the suitability tagging and anonymisation of data. The approach described here offers a response to question two:

> 2. How might the anonymisation and suitability checking of corpus data be approached?

As discussed in Chapter 3, any text or transcript in CorCenCC, across any data mode, that contains language or specific topics/content deemed a sensitive and/or inappropriate for users under the age of 18 was marked up. To do this, the following tag was added at the text level [*rhegi* = to swear or curse]:

<*rhegi* > text </*rhegi*>

An automated script (i.e. computer code/software) was built specifically to support the tagging of the following features (defined as *rhegi*):

- a large list of English profanities (compiled from several lists available online)
- racial, ethnic, homophobic, misogynist and other slurs
- many English words relating to drug use, smoking, alcohol, death, religion and politics
- Welsh equivalents of the above, where these could be identified
- Welsh idiomatic profanities.

The 'blocklist' of words in each of these categories was compiled by searching for openly available lists in English, then searching the CorCenCC lexicon for Welsh words with any of the listed English words given as a translation. Added to this list were headwords from an online Welsh profanity dictionary '*Y Rhegiadur*' (www.rhegiadur. com/). Since there is a likelihood that some features were not captured by this approach, additional spot-checking was carried out to identify further features to be tagged. The *Y Tiwtiadur* website notes while it is impossible to guarantee that all examples/texts *are* suitable for a young audience, 'as far as possible' the majority should be.

The workflow used to carry out suitability tagging and anonymisation differed according to the specific source and type of data included. The most labour-intensive element was the spoken data. During transcription, transcribers were required to include the *<rhegi>* text *</rhegi>* tags where relevant. They were also required to manually substitute the features that make speakers (or referents) and personal information identifiable with appropriate anonymisation tags and, as far as possible, to omit data that was potentially sensitive and/or compromising to the speakers involved, including where:

- it is possible to identify the speaker or anybody they are talking about in the transcript
- there is a potential libel or slander
- it could cause embarrassment (e.g. revealing personal information)
- it could cause someone financial loss (e.g. divulging bank details)
- it could put someone in a compromising position (e.g. discussion of misconduct at work or illegal activities)

- it could cause someone harm in any other way (e.g. divulging passwords).

Transcribers were also asked to inform the research assistant if extensive sections of the transcript included English (and were asked not to transcribe these). All these features were checked as part of the QCing phase described above.

All types of e-language data (i.e. blogs, websites, SMSs and emails) and most written sources (i.e. community newspapers, newsletters, adults' and children's magazines, information brochures and documents and miscellaneous) were subjected to broad quality checks (on formatting, encoding, etc.), automated anonymisation and 'suitability' checking, with at least 25% of the output from the scripts then spot-checked. When extracting some e-language and written texts, the source language of the texts was also reviewed as sometimes entire chapters and/or posts were written in English. While code-switching is a common feature of Welsh-language use, given that the main aim of CorCenCC is to capture contemporary *Welsh*, if extended passages of English text (running to large paragraphs or more) were identified they were removed from the data. 'De-Englishing' was undertaken using an automated script built specifically for this purpose, with at least 25% of the output, again, manually spot-checked by the research team.

Emails and SMSs were processed differently, with 100% manually checked/read to ensure they were appropriately anonymised and tagged for suitability. In addition, published written texts and/or those that are in the public domain or already anonymised (i.e. books—for adults; for children; for learners of the language, journals and essays, coursework and exams), were not anonymised, but were 'de-Englished'. Suitability scripts were not used on these written data types as it was decided that it would be safe to include their contents if texts were already formally published in a children's book or in academic work.

It was considered appropriate to replace personal names with name tags (across all data modes), e.g. <anon> *enwg1* </anon> (first male name in text), rather than providing pseudonyms when anonymising the texts. This decision was made because names, particularly in a minority language context, 'carry a certain amount of social and ethnic information' (Hasund, 1998: 13). Arguably, in the Welsh-language context it may be comparatively easy to guess the name of someone even if you replace their personal name with an alternative name that begins with the same first letter. The names of public figures, public places and/or institutions, celebrities, among others, were not anonymised, but if the speaker was a public figure having a private conversation, names *were* anonymised. The following features were also anonymised: phone numbers, email addresses, personal addresses and postcodes, websites/URLS, business, institution and organisation names, company registration numbers and social media handles (with the first three of these considered as being particularly critical to anonymise—for full details see CorCenCC's transcription conventions in the documentation folder of: https://github.com/CorCenCC).

The automated anonymisation script, as used for some forms of written and e-language data, was only able to handle specific types of patterns. For example, it can recognise that a word with an initial capital letter after the token 'Mr.' is probably a personal name, but it has no way of knowing whether any given word is a name or not unless it is listed in one of the gazetteers of personal names (i.e. the list of names that the script draws on when automatically anonymising). It also cannot predict whether a word is likely to be a nickname. Words that are common in Welsh such as *beth* (= what) and *pam* (= why), but are also names in some cases, will never be anonymised automatically. If data such as postcodes and telephone numbers are typed with errors, e.g. missing digits, or with unusual use of spacing or punctuation, the script does not recognise them. It is hoped that this information was anonymised during manual checking by the researchers, although the project team conceded that it is impossible to ensure 100% accuracy in this process. A contact email address is included on the website so issues relating to the accuracy of anonymisation (among other things) can be reported to the project team.

Tagging

To aid the automatic searching and analysis of corpora, datasets are often also tagged with interpretative linguistic information. A response to question three is provided here:

> **3. What is the purpose of tagging and what features might be useful to tag in corpora?**

The most common, and arguably most useful, features to tag, are the parts-of-speech (POS) of each token in a corpus. Tokens are the smallest unit in a corpus and include words (i.e. items starting with a letter of the alphabet) and nonwords (i.e. items starting with a character that is not a letter of the alphabet). Automated POS taggers have been available for use in many languages for decades. They use pre-defined tagsets (i.e. lists of categories/labels indicative of individual POS) to assign tags to a dataset. Tagsets in various languages are available for reuse here: www.ske tchengine.co.uk/tagsets.

As technology and the availability of extensive corpora (which can be used as data training sets) have proliferated, the accuracy and robustness of POS taggers have also increased. The TreeTagger (Schmid, 1994), for example, tags with a reported accuracy of 96%, while the Standford Log-Linear Part-of-Speech Tagger (Toutanova et al., 2003) has an accuracy of over 97%. These are both probabilistic taggers (i.e. they estimate the probability of a given token to be relevant to a specific category/tag) that require extensive hand-coded training corpora to train and optimise the resources.

In under-resourced and minoritised language contexts, there may be a lack of pre-annotated data available (and sometimes simply a lack of data itself) to train probabilistic taggers, so the development of rule-based taggers is often the alternative approach used to develop these tools. Under the rule-based approach, tags are assigned using pre-defined rules regarding which syntactic categories can typically be co-located in a language. The development of these rules is also a manual and time-consuming process. If you are building a corpus in a major language, it may be possible to reuse an existing POS tagger and/or tagset for your dataset, if not, some consideration to how one might resource the development of a bespoke tagger and/or tagset is needed.

CorCenCC's rule-based POS tagging and tokeniser software (i.e. a tool that breaks down a text into the smallest units of a language), CyTag (pronounced 'kuh-tag', see Neale et al., 2018), was built specifically to support the tagging of Welsh-language data. Early versions of CyTag worked primarily by using the information found in *Eurfa*, the largest open-source, freely available dictionary for Welsh (Donnelly, 2013), to produce a list of possible tags for each word in a Welsh text. This dictionary was supplemented by specific lists of place names, first names and surnames extracted from Wikipedia in CyTag, to provide reference materials for grammatically classifying Welsh-language tokens. The released version of CyTag (used to tag CorCenCC v1.0.0) has some further additions to its lexicon, notably including dialectal variants, colloquialisms and slang terms and non-standard forms (e.g. '*di*—shortened form of *wedi*, used as a preverbal particle for expressing the perfective aspect). Also, the lists of proper nouns have been expanded with specifically Welsh place names and personal names, most of which weren't present in the information initially scraped from Wikipedia.

In early evaluations of the tagger, CyTag achieved accuracy levels of over 95%. The tagset developed is compliant with the Expert Advisory Group on Language Engineering Standards, a standard commonly used when creating digital linguistic software (EAGLES—Sinclair, 1996).

CyTag's tagset includes major syntactic categories (e.g. noun, article, preposition, verb) as well as one category representing unique particles to Welsh and one representing other forms such as abbreviations, acronyms, symbols, digits, etc. The full set of tags covers Welsh morphology based on gender (masculine or feminine), number (singular or plural), person (first, second, third) and tense (past, present, future, etc.). The entire CorCenCC dataset has been tagged by the CyTag tagger using this tagset, so items with a specific POS can be searched via the query tools (see below). The method used to build the tagger can be adapted to other language contexts (see https://github.com/CorCenCC/CyTag and Neale et al., 2018 for details).

In addition to POS tags, a novel Welsh-language semantic annotation system was also developed, to semantically tag all the data in CorCenCC. Examples of categories are:

Hyfryd	[adj. *lovely*]	O4.2+	Substances, materials, objects and equipment > Judgement of appearance
Meddwl	[v. *to think*]	X2.1	Psychological actions, states and processes > Thought, belief
Bwyd	[n. *food*]	F1	Food
Felly	[adv. *so,therefore*]	Z5 and A13.3	Grammatical bin/Degree: booster

This tagger was a modification of the existing UCREL Semantic Analysis System (USAS, Rayson et al., 2004) tagset that, before developments on the CorCenCC project, had been adapted for use (from English) in languages including Malay, Dutch, Russian, Chinese and many others. The semantic tagger/tagset enables users of the corpus to undertake meaning-based queries of the data across, for example, the different genres, topics and modes in the corpus (Piao et al., 2018). Corpus builders are advised to consult the UCREL website to see if a freely available version of the semantic tagger is available for use in their own language, if not, there could be the potential for developing a bespoke tagger by replicating the approaches used in other languages, including Welsh.

Corpus Management Software

A further, important, consideration of the corpus building process, is how (meta)data is managed. Collecting a large amount of varying data types requires appropriate technologies for storing data in an organised and secure manner.

> 4. What are corpus managers and what are they used for?

Corpus managers are digital database tools that support this process. The purpose of corpus managers is, for example, to manage metadata (e.g. integrating information about the source data, authors, topics, genres, etc.), store corpus data and compute statistics (e.g. searching for frequency and distribution features, etc.) (Rychlý, 2007). Examples of existing corpus managers include CQPWeb (Hardie, 2012), Sketch Engine (Kilgarriff et al., 2010) and NoSketch Engine, an open-source (and stripped down) version of Sketch Engine that those with adequate technical abilities can use to build their own corpora (Rychlý, 2007).

CorCenCC's Data Management Tool (a Database Management System—DBMS), a corpus manager, was designed and built to improve the efficiency of handling large quantities of data, as well as to provide a direct link between the data sources and the final corpus as it is accessed by users. This tool is web-based and enables different levels of users to access different aspects of the tool through the same easy-to-use interface (with users not requiring any prior knowledge of the technical aspects of the database). Figure 4.2 shows the main login options and functionalities for users building the CorCenCC dataset.

The basic structure of this tool is invaluable for managing data for corpora of other minority and major world languages too. The tool has the flexibility to enable an individual transcriber (*trawsgrifydd*) to access audio files securely, for the purpose of transcription. In addition to this, the researcher (*ymchwilydd*) can login and, for example, add or update data and gain statistical information about the amount of data collected, with ease. Figure 4.3 shows selected windows of the tool's interface, including adding contributions and raw files (left), assigning and managing transcriptions (middle) and viewing running word counts at every stage of processing (right).

The researcher provides the metadata associated with each uploaded raw data file, categorises it against the design frame, associates the record with its participants by providing a unique contributor ID (assigned to every unique, signed and indexed, consent and speaker/author information form), attaches the data file and then inserts it into the database. Contributions provided through the crowdsourcing app are also accessible to the researcher via this interface, as are provisions for managing the quality checking of transcriptions and data.

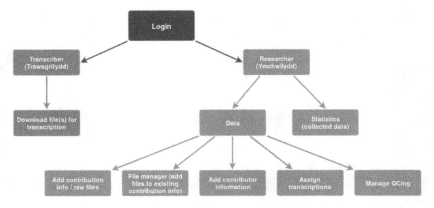

Fig. 4.2 User login options in CorCenCC's database management tool

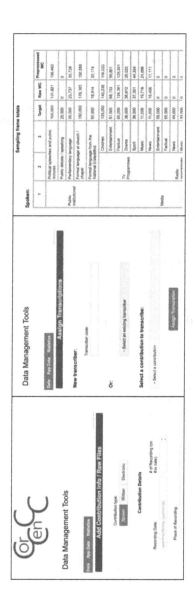

Fig. 4.3 Examples of CorCenCC Data Management Tool interfaces

The data in this tool exists in three different formats. First is the raw data file (i.e. .doc, .txt, PDF or .wav audio recording). Once data has been converted into .txt format, either by file conversion or through transcription, and has been anonymised, it is saved in a 'pre-processed' folder. Once this data has been checked, tagged and fully processed, it is copied (in its revised form) and saved to the 'processed' folder, to be included in the final corpus dataset. This three-stage process is somewhat time consuming, but essential in ensuring the accurate processing and cataloguing of data.

Each individual text is labelled with a 'contribution_ID' when it is uploaded to, and recorded in, the DBMS. Each label includes 17 characters comprising:

Label: mode_initials of researcher_year-month-day_text number for record
Character count: [3 characters]_[2 characters]_[6 characters]_[3 characters]
Example: lla_jn_160922_001

In this example, the contribution labelled 'lla_jn_160922_001' points to a 'spoken' text, recorded by a researcher with the initials 'jn' on 22nd September 2016. '001' at the end indicates that this was the first spoken contribution recorded by 'jn' on that date. The specific modes of data are labelled as *lla* (*llafar*, spoken), *ysg* (*ysgrifenedig*, written) and *ele* (*electronig*, e-language), respectively.

CorCenCC's Data Management Tool also hosts front-end query tools that are used to undertake the analyses of the corpus.

> 5. What are some of the query tools and applications that may be used to facilitate the exploration of corpus data?

Numerous query tools exist which may be used to interrogate a corpus dataset (once it has been built), particularly if the appropriate funding and/or expertise to develop bespoke tools for this purpose do not exist. These tools include AntConc (Anthony, 2020), WMatrix (Rayson, 2002), CQPWeb (Hardie, 2012) and #LancsBox (Brezina et al., 2020), that support, for example, frequency, collocation and keyword analysis as well as the creation of concordance outputs, in a range of languages (these functionalities are discussed below).

A bespoke set of bilingual query tools was created as part of the CorCenCC project. An end user requirements survey was carried out to determine the design of these tools (Knight et al., 2021: 50). Circulated via social media and relevant academic mailing lists (e.g. Corpora List and the British Association for Applied Linguistics' BAALmail list), the survey ascertained what functionalities corpus researchers typically use when querying corpora. The following functionalities were integrated into CorCenCC's query tools because of this survey's results, each will be discussed briefly in turn below:

- Simple Query
- Full Query
- Frequency List
- N-Gram Analysis
- Keyword Analysis
- Collocation Analysis

It should be noted that all of the functionalities in CorCenCC's query tools make calculations based on *tokens*. The examples draw on data from the complete CorCenCC corpus (across all nodes), which contains over 13.4-million-tokens (11.2-million-words—see Chapter 5 for a detailed breakdown of the final corpus dataset). Individual search terms (and their English translations) used to query these tools in these examples are marked in parenthesis, e.g. '*yn*' ('in').

Simple query: This functionality enables users to explore any word and/or lemma in the corpus (i.e. the base/stem form of a word and its inflectional forms), and one or many part-of-speech (POS) tags, mutation types (i.e. the modification of initial consonants in certain grammatical/morphological environments), or semantic category tags of a specific word and/or lemma. A randomised selection of results is presented in a KWIC (Key Word in Context) output once a query has been made. Results can then be filtered by mode, geographical area, context, genre, topic, target audience and source (i.e. the metadata categories defined in Chapter 3). Figure 4.4 provides an example of a KWIC output from a

No.	Mode	Co-text	Word	Co-text
1	Spoken	am tua pump dydd . Un sesiwn ar un dydd a un	dydd	lle ' dw i 'n jest eistedd ar y soffa a gwylio
2	Electronic	gyda Y Bandana a 'l ffefrynnau a gorffen am 1 heno .	Dydd	Sadwrn - Y noson olaf yn nghwmni - Swnami , enwg enw
3	Spoken	cael thirty ? Fi 'n siŵr bod tua tri dag 'ne [saib]	Dydd	Gwener . Oedd llwyth 'na + S1 O really ? S2 +
4	Electronic	penwythnos . Felly gyda iwc , erbyn dydd Llun (neu ddiwedd	dydd	Llun) . Diolch yn fawr . Hwyl , enw2 Popeth yn
5	Electronic	ei thaith hirfaith yn lle _ enwg_ a thrwy fro wledig _ cyfenw_	ddydd	Mawrth . Bydd y daith yn cynnwys nifer o leoliadau siopa lledled
6	Electronic	lle 100 lle Road , Mynydd Bychan , rhif_ffon e-bost Oriau Agor	Dydd	Mawrth i ddydd Sadwrn 10 am - amser pm Copyright 2014 cyfenw
7	Electronic	oherwydd bod yna cymaint o dystiolaeth yn dod i 'r wyneb pob	dydd	ar hyn o bryd am sut mae dynol ryw yn eu annilyr
8	Written	ar ôl ysgol , yn ystod y tymor ac yn ystod y	dydd	dros y gwyliau . Os taw dyma 'r gnŵp oedran rydych eisiau
9	Spoken	Ond dw i erioed 'di clywed am wrthod bwyta yn ystod y	dydd	a jest bwyta yn ystod y nos . S1 Wel na .
10	Electronic	Mae Arddangosfa Tywysogion cyfenw yng Nghanolfan Groeso enwg yn agored bob	dydd	drwy 'r flwyddyn . Yr oriau agor yn ystod y gaeaf yw
11	Electronic	cyfenw cyfenw) . Onid oes lle i lyfrau am 'r redwyr	dydd	Sul ' fel fi ? O 'r diwedd dyma fi 'n cwblhau
12	Written	es i , Emily - Haf enw a enwb _ cyfenw_ ar fore	Dydd	Mercher _dyddiad_ . I 'r Ganolfan i rannu ein hanes . Roedd y
13	Written	? Ddweddiglo 'r hanes yw i ape ' l Oded gario 'r	ddydd	, ac onid oes sawr y Testament Newydd ar yr adnod olaf
14	Spoken	" Cewch chi weld enwb Dydd Sadwrn . Cewch chi weld enwb	Dydd	Sul ' wedyn yyy mwyn cael amrywiaeth < anegiur 3 > Dydd
15	Electronic	pa mor agos ati oeddwn i ... Byxwyd yn 2020	Dydd	- Sul dyddiad 7.00 ." Helo enw . Te neu goffi
16	Spoken	. S1 + Dysgu Cymraeg o bell + S5 O na .	Dydd	Sul yyy dw i ' sio mynd i 'r ffair Nadolig .
17	Electronic	rhwng popeth , felly dim problem . Ddim yn siŵr am brynhawn	dydd	Sadwrn : mae 'n debyg y bydaf yn enw_lleollad ryw ben o
18	Written	00 : 05 DIWEDD / CLOSE Gwybodaeth Rhaglenni Programme Information - S4C	Dydd	Gwener : Friday 18 / 11 / 2016 07 : 00 CYW
19	Written	di dydd Mawrth ? Dydd Llun Dydd Mawrth Dydd Mercher Dydd Iau	Dydd	Gwener 16.2 Esgusodion Atebwch yn ôl yr enghraifft : A : Fyddi
20	Electronic	yn ystod hanner tymor mis dyddiad (dydd Llun dyddiad efor -	dydd	enwb._dyddiad_) ? enwb enwg _lle_ a Jac_ cyfenw_ fydd yn
21	Written	tachwr . Datblygodd bartneriaeth firwython gyda Bryn Jones (Aaron Ramsey ei	ddydd	) with I Murphy ennill y bêl drwy 'r daclo grymus yng
22	Electronic	yn ymuno yn yr Oedfa 'r cyfenw ar faes yr Eisteddfod Genedlaethol	dydd	Sul dyddiad . Yna yn y prynhawn byddwn ym Moreia Tycroes am
23	Written	cyfle i gael profiad o 'r Gymraeg i 'r telel hon o	ddydd	i ddydd yn gyffrous iawn hefyd . Ond rwy 'n credu mai
24	Spoken	o 'r Dydd Iau a rŵan dw i isho bod yno bore	Dydd	Mawrth so siawns i yyy [-] . S1 Ti 'n aros yn
25	Written	fydd yn dod at ei goeid yn ddigon buan i achub 'r	dydd	? .08 : 45 SYRCAS DEITHIOL DEWI : Het Dewi (R
26	Electronic	. Mae 'n benthyg i ni lyfrgell sy 'n todd! 'r	dydd	yn nos . Ac yn ewlle , mae Tŷ Newydd yn
27	Written	'n ceisio darganfod a aeth Jason adref gyda Melissa . I ddathlu	dydd	Miwsig Cymru , mae 'r gnŵp Bendith yn chwaraw gig yn y
28	Electronic	innau a chyfaill yn tynnu lluniau swyddogol Triathlon lle ar dyddiad	dydd	) . Fe fyddant ar gael mor fuan a phosib wedi
29	Spoken	'di mynd yn confused a dw i 'n edrach arnyn nhw bob	dydd	< S ? > naill ai ddim mirina neu jest yn gwbod
30	Written	llawn trugareddau o bob math : deihyddidau sidan lliwgar na welsant olau	dydd	ers blynyddoedd ; brodwaith bendigedig fy Nain Sowth mewn bag plastig

Fig. 4.4 KWIC output for 'dydd' in CorCenCC (30 random instances from 11,057)

simple query of CorCenCC. Queried here, across all three modes (with individual modes indicated by the second column), is '*dydd*' ('day').

The search term (Word) is presented in the middle of the screenshot here, with the extended left and right 'Co-text' of each instance of use also presented. The differences in colour of tokens (as seen in the online output) map to specific POS tags for each token in the corpus. '*Dydd*' occurs 11,057 times in the corpus, with a relative frequency of 0.08% (calculated as the percentage rate of use of a item relative to the entire dataset—i.e. 13,487,210 tokens in the case of CorCenCC). Welsh days of the week all start with '*Dydd*', e.g. '*Dydd Sadwrn*' > 'Saturday' and there are several examples of this in the figure, from all three modes of data (i.e. lines 2–6 and 11–12). About half of the examples relate to specific days of the week but in line 27 there is a reference to '*Dydd Miwsig Cymru*' ('Welsh Music Day') an annual event that celebrates all forms of Welsh-language music. Other uses of '*dydd*' include common fixed phrases, e.g. in lines 8 and 9 there is the use of '*yn ystod y dydd*' ('during the day'), '*pob dydd*' ('every day') in lines 10 and 29 and '*o ddydd i ddydd*' ('from day to day') in line 23. '*Bore*' precedes '*dydd*' to give an 'Xday morning' in lines 12 and 24.

Full Query: This functionality is used to search for longer sequences of patterns separated by spaces (i.e. multi-word expressions), using CorCenCC's bespoke query syntax. Results are again presented in a KWIC output, that can be filtered according to the metadata categories defined in Chapter 3. The syntax used in CorCenCC is loosely based on the query syntax used in CQPweb (see https://cqpweb.lancs.ac.uk/ and Hardie, 2012). Specific details of this syntax can be found on the full query tab in CorCenCC's corpus query tools.

Frequency List: A typical way to querying a corpus, if no specific search terms are pre-defined, is to create a frequency list. This produces a list of words or lemmas in the corpus, according to their frequency of occurrence. Frequency lists profile the items most commonly used in a language, effectively underlining the 'nuts and bolts' of that language. Table 4.1, a screenshot of the frequency list functionality, details the 20 most frequent words in CorCenCC.

The first column of this table (No.) provides the frequency-related order of each word in the corpus—from the most frequent to the least (with the top 20 tabulated here), followed by the word itself (column 2—Word). This is followed by the tagged part-of-speech (POS) of the

Table 4.1 Top 20 most frequent words in CorCenCC (across all modes)

No	Word	POS	Count	Frequency (%)
1	Yn	Arsym	520,461	3.86%
2	Y	YFB	317,835	2.36%
3	'r	YFB	267,947	1.99%
4	i	Arsym	229,542	1.70%
5	a	Cyscyd	226,472	1.68%
6	o	Arsym	206,657	1.53%
7	ar	Arsym	152,892	1.13%
8	Mae	Bpres3u	146,070	1.08%
9	i	Rhaperslu	122,700	0.91%
10	'n	Uberf	119,726	0.89%
11	'n	Utra	85,444	0.63%
12	ac	Cyscyd	84,634	0.63%
13	yr	YFB	83,755	0.62%
14	am	Arsym	68,471	0.51%
15	a	Arsym	63,389	0.47%
16	ond	Arsym	58,206	0.43%
17	wedi	Uberf	57,653	0.43%
18	bod	Be	55,727	0.41%
19	ni	Rhaperslll	53,683	0.40%
20	ei	Rhadib3gu	48,262	0.36%

word, the number of times it occurs in CorCenCC (Count) and its relative frequency (Frequency). As with other corpora, a certain amount of researcher engagement is required to check/scrutinise outputs such as is presented here (to interpret them effectively). This is because analytical tools may count certain features of a language, or mark-up, that a user may not always equate to being a 'word', e.g. tags or features of transcription, that, if not of interest, may need to be removed from outputs as data is explored in more detail.

An example of this in Table 4.1 is the most frequent word '*Yn*'. The POS tags used in CorCenCC are abbreviations of their Welsh-language forms, e.g. YFB > *Y Fannod Benodol* = The Definite Article. '*Yn*' here has the POS '*Arsym*' (simple preposition). The Welsh word '*yn*' however fulfils three principal roles in the language:

    i. As a simple preposition corresponding to English 'in' + a definite noun: *Mae Mari yn y siop* (Mari is in the shop)

ii. A verb particle with the POS *Uberf* (unique verb particle): *Mae Dafydd yn prynu bwyd* (Dafydd is buying food)

iii. A predicative particle *Utra: Mae'r bwyd yn flasus* (The food is delicious)

A wider analysis of this particular item can be found in Knight et al. (2020a), with reference to the creation of *Yr Amliadur* (frequency lists developed from the CorCenCC corpus, Knight et al., 2020b). This illustrates that designing taggers that can completely disambiguate word usages can be a challenge in any language.

Another example is the terms listed 2nd, 3rd and 13th which give different forms of the Welsh definite article. The default article '*y*' is listed 2nd with the form '*r*', used after a vowel, 3rd. '*Y*' changes to '*Yr*' when followed by a vowel or h+vowel and this is 13th on the frequency list in Table 4.1. Otherwise, in the Welsh frequency list's top 20 words, prepositions and particles predominate except for:

i. First person singular and plural pronouns '*i*' and '*ni*'

ii. The third person singular present '*mae*' ('is') and its verb-noun form '*bod*' ('to be') and

iii. The third person singular masculine dependent pronoun '*ei*'

Therefore, in a similar way to English, and perhaps most other languages, function words proliferate over content words here. These words provide the mechanics of the language, structuring and organising it.

To examine content words in more detail, scrutinising the POS tags in CorCenCC's search query tool of the frequency list functionality can help. A starting point for this might be, for example, to examine the most frequent masculine ('*Egu*') and feminine ('*Ebu*') nouns in the corpus. Specific forms of lemma, mutation and lists of the most common words in a semantic category can also be defined by adjusting the search queries in this tool.

N-Gram Analysis: In a similar way to the frequency list functionality, the n-gram analysis identifies patterns of lists of 2–7 words, lemmas or POS clusters (i.e. n-grams) in the corpus, according to their frequency of occurrence.

Keyword Analysis: The keyword analysis functionality (based on 'keyness' scores, Scott & Tribble, 2006), provides statistical comparisons of

4 PROCESSING AND (RE)PRESENTING CORPORA   129

frequencies between a target (i.e. the sub-dataset of interest, perhaps pertaining to a specific genre, context or other variable) and reference (a broader, typically bigger, dataset that provides a baseline against which the target is compared) corpus, calculated using the log-likelihood measure. Positive keyness, represented by '+' log-likelihood values, are words, phrases and/or themes that are used at a significantly higher frequency in a target corpus (with a p value <0.01, and a critical value range of >6.63) compared to a reference corpus, while negative keyness scores, represented by '−' log-likelihood values, are those terms that are used at a significantly lower rate in the target corpus. Keyness analyses of patterns in the use of words, POS and themes, as is offered by CorCenCC, allow for the identification of phenomena that emerge as being particularly characteristic and/or significant of a corpus under examination.

Collocation Analysis: This functionality displays information on the relationships between words that appear together within a given context window (i.e. items that commonly co-occur together). Table 4.2 provides an example of the results obtained from a collocation search of '*gyfer*' ('direction'), the soft mutated form of the 5th most common noun ('*cyfer*') in the CorCenCC corpus across all modes (at $n-/+1$, i.e. within the context window of one word to each side of the search term ('n'), '*gyfer*').

The search output indicates that there are 2021 collocates of '*gyfer*'. The most common collocate of '*gyfer*' is '*ar*', which occurs 14,443 times (see Count column), i.e. a rate of 99.24% (Freq. (with '*gyfer*')) at $n-/+1$. A more refined search of this term, at $n - 1$, indicates that in 100% of these cases these collocates in fact have the pattern of '*ar gyfer*', i.e. with '*ar*' preceding the noun. The results shown here have been sorted by the values in the 4th column, that is the percentage-based frequency of the patterns of co-occurring words (rather than the overall frequency of the collocate, which would be determined if the table were sorted according to the first column, No.).

Detailed in the 'Rank' column in Table 4.2 is the Mutual Information score, MI, for each collocate. The MI score denotes the statistical dependence of co-occurring words (i.e. the *strength of association*), and whether the rate of co-occurrence is higher than would be expected by chance. In more detailed analysis/descriptions of language use patterns one should consider both the strength of association and frequency of co-occurrence to gain a full understanding of the patterns seen as there is not always a 1:1 mapping between these values.

Table 4.2 Collocates of '*gyfer*' at $n-/+1$, listed according to the frequency of co-occurrence

No	Collocate	Count	Freq. (with 'gyfer', %)	Freq. (total, %)	Rank
245	ar	14,443	99.24%	0.11%	5.4517
1077	y	2842	19.53%	0.02%	1.9187
1148	yr	630	4.33%	0.00%	1.6811
372	plant	432	2.97%	0.00%	4.5931
424	pob	299	2.05%	0.00%	4.2430
1508	ei	248	1.70%	0.00%	0.3726
683	eich	241	1.66%	0.00%	3.1499
862	ein	228	1.57%	0.00%	2.5804
549	S4C	187	1.28%	0.00%	3.6337
1297	eu	179	1.23%	0.00%	1.2287
670	pobl	158	1.09%	0.00%	3.1765
374	popeth	134	0.92%	0.00%	4.5829
997	unrhyw	107	0.74%	0.00%	2.1736
1467	Cymru	99	0.68%	0.00%	0.5149
778	cyfnod	64	0.44%	0.00%	2.8368
924	rhaglen	60	0.41%	0.00%	2.3647
1761	un	57	0.39%	0.00%	−0.7788
1536	Fy	53	0.36%	0.00%	0.2744
155	darparwyr	49	0.34%	0.00%	6.5224
710	datblygu	50	0.34%	0.00%	3.0596

Y Tiwtiadur

Unique to the CorCenCC corpus is an additional set of query tools with a specific user group in mind: teachers and learners. *Y Tiwtiadur* (https://ytiwtiadur.corcencc.org) is a set of digital teaching and learning tools that were built to work directly with the full corpus dataset. The tools were inspired by the Compleat Lexical Tutor (www.lextutor.ca/— with the developer of this toolkit, Cobb, providing consultative advice to the project), one of the highest profile and frequently accessed (c.15,000 users p/day) online English-language resources.

Y Tiwtiadur was built based on the concept of Data-Driven Learning (DDL), a semi-autonomous approach to learning, where learners are encouraged to inspect instances of language use to gain a deeper understanding of the mechanics of it. *Y Tiwtiadur* enables the learner to examine how their target language is actually used in practice, in a variety of contexts and genres (see Knight et al., 2020a). Integrating learning

4 PROCESSING AND (RE)PRESENTING CORPORA 131

resources into CorCenCC's bespoke query tools enables learners to access relevant corpus data in a directed way and obviates the need for explicit training in corpus methods, that may be time consuming and demotivating. *Υ Tiwtiadur* features the following tools: gap-fill, word profiler, word identification and word task creator.

Figure 4.5 provides screenshot examples of *Υ Tiwtiadur*'s word identifier functionality. In the top image, the user has chosen to create a task that draws on examples from the Level 1000 frequency band (i.e. the 1000 most frequent words in Welsh, as evidenced by CorCenCC), with a selected focus on 'the definite article' (*y fannod benodol*), and a maximum of five sentences. The output is shown in the second image, a word identifying task with the missing word meeting the specified requirements. The task for the learner is to correctly guess which word fits the 'gap' in this output.

A technical account of the design of both CorCenCC's corpus query tools and *Υ Tiwtiadur* can be found in Knight et al. (2020a, 2021) respectively. The discussions presented in this present chapter function to illustrate some of the ways in which corpora can be processed, (re)presented and queried. The final pieces of the corpus design puzzle now need to be put in place: the 'results' of the corpus design methodology, and a critical reflection of the final composition of CorCenCC. These are provided in the next chapter.

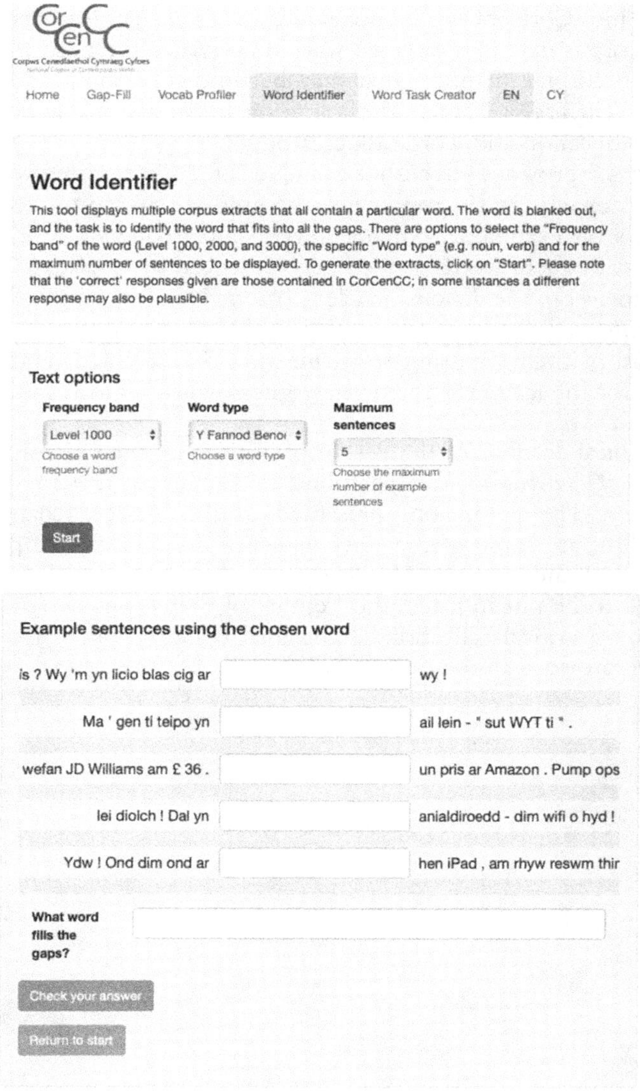

Corpws Cenedlaethol Cymraeg Cyfoes
Home
Gap-Fill
Vocab Profiler
Word Identifier
Word Task Creator
EN
CY
Word Identifier
This tool displays multiple corpus extracts that all contain a particular word. The word is blanked out, and the task is to identify the word that fits into all the gaps. There are options to select the "Frequency band" of the word (Level 1000, 2000, and 3000), the specific "Word type" (e.g. noun, verb) and for the maximum number of sentences to be displayed. To generate the extracts, click on "Start". Please note that the 'correct' responses given are those contained in CorCenCC; in some instances a different response may also be plausible.
Text options
Frequency band
Level 1000
Choose a word frequency band
Word type
Y Fannod Benoı
Choose a word type
Maximum sentences
5
Choose the maximum number of example sentences
Start
Example sentences using the chosen word
is ? Wy 'm yn licio blas cig ar
wy !
Ma ' gen ti teipo yn
ail lein - " sut WYT ti " .
wefan JD Williams am £ 36 .
un pris ar Amazon . Pump ops
lei diolch ! Dal yn
anialdiroedd - dim wifi o hyd !
Ydw ! Ond dim ond ar
hen iPad , am rhyw reswm thir
What word fills the gaps?
Check your answer
Return to start

Fig. 4.5 Word identifier functionality in CorCenCC's *Y Tiwtiadur*

References

Anderson, J., Beavan, D., & Kay, C. (2007). SCOTS: Scottish corpus of texts and speech. In J. Beal, K. Corrigan, & H. Moisl (Eds.), *Creating and digitizing language corpora: Volume 1—Synchronic databases* (pp. 17–34). Palgrave Macmillan.

Anthony, L. (2020). *AntConc (Version 3.5.9)* [Software]. Waseda University. Retrieved from https://www.laurenceanthony.net/software [Accessed 20/06/2021].

Aston, G., & Burnard, L. (1997). *The BNC handbook: Exploring the British national corpus with SARA*. Edinburgh University Press.

Atkins, S., Clear, J., & Ostler, N. (1992). Corpus design criteria. *Literary and Linguistic Computing, 7*(1), 1–16.

Biber, D., Johansson, S., Leech, G., Conrad, S., & Finegan, E. (1999). *Longman grammar of spoken and written English*. Longman, Pearson.

Brezina, V., Weill-Tessier, P., & McEnery, A. (2020). *#LancsBox v. 5.x*. [Software]. Lancaster University. Retrieved from http://corpora.lancs.ac.uk/lancsbox [Accessed 20/06/2021].

Deuchar, M., Webb-Davies, P., & Donnelly, K. (2018). *Building and using the Siarad corpus*. John Benjamins.

Donnelly, K. (2013). *Eurfa v3.0—Free (GPL) dictionary (incorporating Konjugator and Rhymer)* [Online]. Retrieved from: http://eurfa.org.uk [Accessed 20/06/2021].

Edwards, J. (1995). Principles and alternative systems in the transcription, coding and mark-up of spoken discourse. In G. Leech, G. Myers, & J. Thomas (Eds.), *Spoken English on computer: Transcription, mark-up and application* (pp. 19–34). Longman.

Hardie, A. (2012). CQPweb—Combining power, flexibility and usability in a corpus analysis tool. *International Journal of Corpus Linguistics, 17*, 380–409.

Hasund, K. (1998). Protecting the innocent: The issue of informants' anonymity in the COLT corpus. In A. Renouf (Ed.), *Explorations in corpus linguistics* (pp. 13–28). Rodopi.

Kilgarriff, A., Reddy, S., Pomikálek, J., & Avinesh, P. V. S. (2010). A corpus factory for many languages. In *Proceedings of the Language Resources and Evaluation (LREC)* (pp. 904–910). Valetta, Malta.

Knight, D., Morris, S., Fitzpatrick, T., Rayson, P., Spasić, I., & Môn Thomas, E. (2020a). *The national corpus of contemporary Welsh: Project report|Y corpws cenedlaethol Cymraeg cyfoes: adroddiad y prosiect*. Retrieved from http://orca.cf.ac.uk/135540/ [Accessed 20/06/2021].

Knight, D., Morris, S., Tovey-Walsh, B., & Fitzpatrick, T. (2020b). *Yr Amliadur: Frequency lists for contemporary Welsh*. Cardiff University. https://doi.org/10.17035/d.2020.0120164107 [Accessed 20/06/2021].

Knight, D., Morris, S., & Fitzpatrick, T. (2021). *Corpus design and construction in minoritised language contexts: The national corpus of contemporary Welsh.* Palgrave.

Love, R., Dembry, C., Hardie, A., Brezina, V., & McEnery, T. (2017a). The spoken BNC 2014: Designing and building a spoken corpus of everyday conversations. *International Journal of Corpus Linguistics, 22*, 319–344.

Love, R., Hawtin, A., & Hardie, A. (2017b). *The British national corpus 2014: User manual and reference guide (version 1.0).* Retrieved from: http://corpora.lancs.ac.uk/bnc2014/doc/BNC2014manual.pdf [Accessed 20/06/2021].

MacWhinney, B. (2000). The CHILDES project: Tools for analyzing talk. *Child Language Teaching and Therapy, 8*(2), 217–218.

McCarthy, M. J. (1998). *Spoken language and applied linguistics.* Cambridge University Press.

Neale, S., Donnelly, K., Watkins, G., & Knight, D. (2018). Leveraging lexical resources and constraint grammar for rule-based part-of-speech tagging in Welsh. In *Proceedings of the LREC (Language Resources Evaluation) 2018 Conference* (pp. 3946–3954). Miyazaki, Japan.

O'Keeffe, A., McCarthy, M. J., & Carter, R. (2007). *From corpus to classroom: Language use and language teaching.* Cambridge University Press.

Piao, S., Rayson, P., Knight, D., & Watkins, G. (2018). Towards a Welsh semantic annotation system. In *Proceedings of the LREC (Language Resources Evaluation Conference)* (pp. 980–985). Miyazaki, Japan.

Rayson, P. (2002). *Matrix: A statistical method and software tool for linguistic analysis through corpus comparison.* Unpublished Ph.D. thesis, Lancaster University.

Rayson, P., Archer, D., Piao, S., & McEnery, T. (2004). The UCREL semantic analysis system. In *Proceedings of the Language Resources and Evaluation (LREC)* (pp. 7–12). Lisbon, Portugal.

Reppen, R. (2010). Building a corpus. In A. O'Keeffe & M. J. McCarthy (Eds.), *The Routledge handbook of corpus linguistics* (pp. 31–37). Routledge.

Rychlý, P. (2007). Manatee/Bonito—A modular corpus manager. *Proceedings of RASLAN (Recent Advances in Slavonic Natural Language Processing)* (pp. 65–70). Masaryk University, Brno, Czechia.

Schmid, H. (1994). Probabilistic part-of-speech tagging using decision trees. *Proceedings of the International Conference on New Methods in Language Processing* (pp. 44–49). Manchester.

Schmidt, T. (2016). Good practices in the compilation of FOLK, the research and teaching corpus of spoken German. *International Journal of Corpus Linguistics, 21*(3), 396–418.

Scott, M., & Tribble, C. (2006). *Textual patterns: Key words and corpus analysis in language education.* John Benjamins.

4 PROCESSING AND (RE)PRESENTING CORPORA 135

Sinclair, J. (1987). Collocation: A progress report. In R. Steele & T. Threadgold (Eds.), *Language topics: Essays in honour of Michael Halliday* (pp. 319–331). John Benjamins.

Sinclair, J. (1996). *EAGLES preliminary recommendations on corpus typology* [Online]. Retrieved from http://www.ilc.cnr.it/EAGLES96/corpustyp/corpustyp.html [Accessed 20/06/2021].

Sperberg-McQueen, C., & Burnard, L. (1993). *Guidelines for electronic text encoding and interchange (TEI P3)* [Online]. Retrieved from https://tei-c.org/Vault/GL/p4beta.pdf [Accessed 20/06/2021].

Tagliamonte, S. A. (2007). Representing real language: Consistency, trade-offs and thinking ahead! In J. Beal, K. Corrigan, & H. Moisl (Eds.), *Creating and digitizing language corpora: Synchronic databases* (Vol. 1, pp. 205–240). Palgrave Macmilan.

Toutanova, K., Klein, D., Manning, C., & Singer, Y. (2003). Feature-rich part-of-speech tagging with a cyclic dependency network. In *Proceedings of HLT-NAACL 2003* (pp. 173–180). Edmonton.

Wittenburg, P., Brugman, H., Russel, A., Klassmann, A., & Sloetjes, H. (2006). ELAN: A professional framework for multimodality research. *Proceedings of the Fifth International Conference on Language Resources and Evaluation (LREC 2006)* (pp. 1556–1559). Genoa, Italy.

Woods, D., & Fassnacht, C. (2007). *Transana* [Software]. Retrieved from https://www.transana.com [Accessed 20/06/2021].

Wörner, K., & Schmidt, T. (2009). EXMARaLDA—Creating, analysing and sharing spoken language corpora for pragmatic research. *Pragmatics, 19*(4), 565–582.

CHAPTER 5

Results, Reflections and Lessons Learnt

Abstract This chapter details the final composition of each of CorCenCC's sub-corpora, reflects on some of the practical issues and challenges faced when compiling these sub-corpora, and assesses the relative similarity (and differences) of the released corpus in comparison to its initial design (as presented in Chapter 2). The chapter effectively presents the 'results' of our approach to building a corpus, by critically evaluating the final dataset. The presentation of these results helps to signpost some of the key lessons learnt from our experiences of building CorCenCC, lessons that can be adapted for use in other language contexts. This chapter and book end with some examples of the sorts of questions that a national corpus like CorCenCC might be used to answer.

Keywords Corpus composition · Contributor demographics · Categorisation · Text variability · Contributor engagement · Quality control · Consent

OVERVIEW

As underlined in Chapter 2, while a considerable amount of time was dedicated to the development of CorCenCC's design frames, as with all other corpus design frames, these exist as prototypes. It is often the case

© The Author(s), under exclusive license to Springer Nature Switzerland AG 2021
D. Knight et al., *Building a National Corpus*,
https://doi.org/10.1007/978-3-030-81858-6_5

137

that the resultant corpus dataset differs (sometimes quite dramatically) from its initial design. In this chapter the 'results' of the endeavours of the WP1 (Work Package 1) team on the CorCenCC project are provided, by:

i. Detailing the final composition of each sub-corpus
ii. Reflecting on some of the practical issues and challenges faced when compiling these sub-corpora and
iii. Assessing the relative similarity (and differences) of the released corpus in comparison to its initial design.

The presentation of these results helps to signpost some of the key lessons learnt from our experiences of building CorCenCC, lessons that can be adapted for use in other contexts. For ease of comparison with Chapter 2, each data mode is tackled in turn here. This structure also enables readers to focus either on a specific mode of language that may be of interest to them or, collectively, to obtain a holistic overview, relevant to those building their own *general* (or national) corpus in any language. This chapter and book end with some examples of the sorts of questions that a national corpus like CorCenCC might be used to answer.

Spoken Data in CorCenCC

CorCenCC's spoken sub-corpus extends to 1331 texts, amounting to 2,864,974 words and comprises 26% of the final full dataset (which contains circa 11.2-million-words). The amounts discussed in this section, and the rest of this chapter, are based on *word* counts from the publicly available CorCenCC dataset (rather than *token* counts—see Chapter 4).

While the initial plan was for 4-million-words of spoken data to be collected, as the project progressed, it became clear that it would not be practical to collect and transcribe this amount of data with the resources available, and within the project's timeframe. How easy was it to develop our spoken corpus? Not easy. The initial data collection plans for the corpus were overambitious. Some of the key issues encountered were as follows (others are discussed in more depth in the sections below):

5 RESULTS, REFLECTIONS AND LESSONS LEARNT 139

- **Sourcing data**: it was particularly difficult to source data from transactional and private contexts, as contributors were wary of providing their permission to be recorded.
- **Converting 'interest' to data**: while many potential participants showed their interest in contributing to the corpus, converting this interest to actual contributions was not always successful. Individuals often ignored correspondence or, particularly with app users, just did not record or upload their data.
- **Transcription challenges**: although a large team of 180 transcribers was recruited to the project, these individuals were not working full time, or even at the same time, so the prompt return of transcriptions was not always guaranteed. The training of transcribers also took more time than initially anticipated, which had a knock-on effect on the turnaround time for completing transcriptions. A few recordings were not transcribed in time to be included in the corpus.
- **Quality control**: the requirement to check the transcriptions (Chapter 3) was vital to maximise the accuracy of the data. However, this additional stage added further delays to the processing of the spoken data.

These issues are not necessarily context-specific, so are likely to be encountered when building spoken corpora in other languages. It is wise to not be too ambitious in your aims from the start.

The weighting/proportions of each sub-corpus were adjusted to reflect these ongoing challenges, with an aim to instead collect a baseline of at least 2-million-words of spoken data. This was achieved. The sub-corpus is categorised according to the contexts and genres detailed in Table 5.1. Note that the specific tags, and the formatting of these, used in this table are consistent with those used in the released version of the corpus, for ease of reference.

Based on feedback from future user groups, and for clarity of description, three of the context tags have been relabelled in the final corpus: 'media' is now 'broadcast', 'pedagogic' is 'educational' and 'socialising' is 'social'. Similarly, some of the specific category labels have been changed, to make them more meaningful and easier for users to interpret and search. Table 5.1 indicates that there are at least 200,000 words in each spoken context, with 'broadcast' including the highest word count (433,361) and 'transactional' the lowest (204,758). While there is not a consistent balance of words across the contexts, it can be argued that

Table 5.1   Composition of CorCenCC's spoken sub-corpus

Context[former tag]	Original target words (% total)	Actual words (% total)	Genres(Additional contexts in italics, as relevant)	Texts	Words
public_or_institutional	400,000 (10%)	433,361 (15.10%)	lecture	12	66,769
			prayer	1	85
			presentation	27	140,042
			proceedings	41	29,495
			sermon	32	169,267
			speech	24	27,703
broadcast [media]	600,000 (15%)	750,078 (26.20%)	radio_programme	132	363,006
			tv_programme	432	387,072
transactional	400,000 (10%)	204,758 (7.10%)	conversation	3	660
			*food_and_drink*_conversation	32	25,078
			*leisure*_conversation	9	16,742
			*public_sector_or_third_sector*_conversation	29	51,416
			*retail_and_services*_conversation	109	92,731
			*tourism_and_travel*_conversation	9	18,131
professional	400,000 (10%)	477,983 (16.7%)	conversation	48	168,408
			meeting	15	160,096
			staff_training_seminar	17	149,479
educational [pedagogic]	400,000 (10%)	296,709 (10.37%)	class_or_tutorial	119	195,866
			lecture	16	97,144
			presentation	1	3699
social [socialising]	900,000 (22.5%)	456,487 (15.9%)	conversation	131	456,487
private	900,000 (22.5%)	245,598 (8.6%)	conversation	89	244,862
			phone_call	3	736
				1331	2,864,974

5 RESULTS, REFLECTIONS AND LESSONS LEARNT   141

200,000 words provide enough data to give useful insights into language use.

Data from 'public' or 'institutional' contexts accounts for 15.10% of the spoken sub-corpus. The original target (Table 2.1) was to collect 150,000 words from 'formal language at the church and chapel'. Table 5.1 indicates that the genres 'prayer' and 'sermon', that represent this category, collectively amount to 169,352 words (39% of the 'public' or 'institutional' context). When collecting data it became apparent that the category of 'parliamentary language' was too vague and difficult to define, so there was no language collected for that category. The category of 'political speeches and public lectures' was also replaced with more specific genres including 'lecture', 'presentation' and 'speech'. The vague category of 'formal language from the National *Eisteddfod*' was replaced by the more clearly defined genre 'proceedings', with some texts collected here classified under the genres of 'presentations' and 'lectures'. There was an original aim to amass 1.25% of the 4-million-word target in this category (50,000 words). At 1.03% of the 2.86-million-word total (29,495 words), this % target was approximately met.

More data than originally planned was collected from the 'broadcast' context. The distribution of TV to radio programmes, mainly sourced from S4C and *Radio Cymru*, respectively, is 52:48. This is not quite the targeted split of 60:40, but it is close. A breakdown of TV and radio programmes is shown in Table 5.2. In some instances, programmes were difficult to classify as one single genre, so multiple genres were used. A text classified as, for example, 'tv_programme'; 'factual'; 'music', is principally 'factual' rather than simply 'music', unlike a text classified as 'music', which is simply music-focused. The broad range of genres featured here somewhat maps to the original targets in Table 2.3, although no commercial/community radio was captured in the corpus, as despite efforts to collect this data, it was not possible to obtain appropriate permission to use this data. Again, some category labels have changed (e.g. 'religion and ethics' is now 'religion'), for the sake of clarity and consistency across sub-corpora, facilitating cross-mode comparisons of the genres.

The items italicised in the 'transactional' context in Table 5.1 have been defined as contexts rather than genres, as for example, '*food_and_drink*' relates to the specific context in which the interaction is taking place, not the distinct rhetorical structure of the text. The highest proportion of texts in this category was from '*retail_and_services*' contexts (92,731 words) rather than '*public_sector_or_third_sector*'

142   D. KNIGHT ET AL.

Table 5.2   Genres in the CorCenCC's spoken 'broadcast' data

Genre(s)			Texts	Words	Totals
tv_programme	childrens_television		227	126,467	432 Texts 387,072 Words
	drama		24	30,607	
	entertainment	entertainment	7	3804	
		factual	67	87,848	
		music	24	23,801	
	factual	factual	41	52,723	
		music	3	2571	
		news_and_weather	3	3650	
	music		3	590	
	news_and_weather		10	14,614	
	sport		23	40,397	
radio_programme	radio_programme		20	98,648	132 Texts 363,006 Words
	entertainment	entertainment	21	49,723	
		comedy	1	189	
		music	11	18,754	
		sport_comedy	1	3825	
	factual	factual	28	66,605	
		news_and_weather	7	19,770	
		sport	1	2889	
	music	music	10	18,959	
		news_and_weather	4	18,415	
	news_and_weather		10	38,107	
	religion		8	9423	
	sport	sport	9	14,356	
		music	1	3343	

contexts (51,416 words). It was particularly challenging to collect data in this latter context: while there was a lot of interest from potential contributors, obtaining the appropriate consent to record data in these contexts proved difficult.

Similarly, collecting data in a range of 'professional' contexts was challenging. For example, despite persistent attempts from the research team, it was not possible to gain consent to record business or phone calls. Similarly, no consent was received to record interviews. The final corpus does, however, include communication in three different genres: 'conversation', 'meeting', 'staff training seminar', with nearly 150,000 words in each (Table 5.1), providing a sound foundation for characterising and examining professional language use.

5 RESULTS, REFLECTIONS AND LESSONS LEARNT   143

The number of words in the 'educational' context meets the original target set (i.e. 10% of the spoken sub-corpus), as seen in Table 5.3.

Two-thirds of these texts are taken from class or tutorial genres, with circa one-third from lectures (and one presentation). Twenty-one of the 'educational' texts were recorded in a first language context (i.e. in a Welsh-medium school: 65,278 words), with 11 in a second language context (25,980 words). The remainder have no specified context. These have also been sub-classified, detailing the specific *genres* of the texts, the *topics* covered by them, the *locations* in which they were recorded and *who* specific recordings involved/conversations were between.

Tables 5.4 and 5.5 provide details of data captured in 'social' and 'private' contexts. The relationships between the speakers in these two contexts are more specific than in the original design frames. On occasion, it was difficult to distinguish between, for example, friends and colleagues, which is why multiple categories exist in some cases. This is a potential limitation of the taxonomy.

A range of locations is represented across these contexts, with the highest number of 'social' data sampled from 'public spaces' and 'pubs, bars, restaurants or cafes' (226,845 words), and in the 'home' in 'private' contexts (238,897 words). These locations appropriately align to where one would typically expect social and private interaction to occur.

A closer look at the demographics of the contributors to the spoken sub-corpus indicates that there were 903 contributors, 811 of whom were individuals and 92 were groups/companies (the latter of whom provided no demographic information). Of the individual contributors, 307 were female (59.4% of those who noted a gender), 209 male (40.5%), one preferred not to say, while 294 provided no response to this question. These percentages mirror the last census results, where the majority of speakers of Welsh were female (53.4–46.6% male, ONS, 2011). Figure 5.1 and Table 5.6 detail the age and location of individual speakers, respectively.

Figure 5.1 indicates that while there is a slight overrepresentation of speakers in the 30–39 category, and an under-representation of those aged 20–29, overall the speakers who contributed to CorCenCC's spoken sub-corpus represent a broad range of ages. Table 5.6 indicates that the highest numbers of contributors came from Carmarthenshire, Cardiff, Swansea, Rhondda Cynon Taf and Gwynedd (in boldface—collectively representing 67.79% of contributors who recorded this information). This distribution broadly reflects the number of Welsh speakers in local

Table 5.3　Composition of CorCenCC's spoken 'educational' data

Genre	Topic	Location	Who	Texts	Words
class_or_tutorial	art_drama_music	secondary_school		5	3117
	humanities	college_or_university; higher_education_institution		1	8905
		secondary_school		16	15,581
	science_and_the_natural_world	secondary_school	students, teachers	19	31,071
		college_or_university; further_education_institution		30	5818
	Welsh_language [first language]	secondary_school	students, teachers	10	9225
		college_or_university; further_education_institution		1	4679
		college_or_university; higher_education_institution		4	13,744
	Welsh_language [second language]	college_or_university; adult_education_institution	students, teachers	11	25,980
	—	primary_school		12	20,123
	—	college_or_university; adult_education_institution	students	1	8183
				4	31,760
	—	college_or_university; further_education_institution		2	9055
	—	college_or_university; higher_education_institution	teachers	3	8625
lecture	Welsh_language [first language]	college_or_university; higher_education_institution	teachers	6	37,630
	humanities		students, teachers	1	9279
	—		teachers	6	33,869
	—		—	3	16,366
presentation		primary_school		1	3699
				136	296,709

Table 5.4 Breakdown of the 'social' data in CorCenCC

Genre	Location	Who	Texts	Words
conversation	—	—	1	425
		friends; society_or_club_members	1	1340
		society_or_club_members	1	12,602
		family	1	52
	National_Eisteddfod	—	1	2227
		friends	17	45,600
	Urdd_Eisteddfod	family	1	2666
		family; friends	3	9255
		family; parents_and_offspring	2	4782
		family; spouses_and_partners	1	1109
		friends	1	2433
	home	friends	1	4664
	public_space	friends	1	6303
		family; friends	1	4459
		family	1	1095
		society_or_club_members	7	27,096
	public_space_event	—	2	3537
		friends	8	10,701
		family; spouses_and_partners	1	834
		family	1	866
		society_or_club_members	1	156
	public_space; library_or_ community_centre	society_or_club_members	13	74,490
	public_space; pub_bar_ restaurant_or_cafe	—	1	4560
		family	3	9841
		friends	25	100,573
		family; friends	2	10,614
		family; parents_and_offspring	1	3882
		friends; colleagues	3	10,288
		society_or_club_members	10	87,087

(continued)

146   D. KNIGHT ET AL.

Table 5.4   (continued)

Genre	Location	Who	Texts	Words
	public_space; shop	colleagues	12	2379
		society_or_club_members	2	6444
	public_space; town_or_city_centre	—	5	4127
			131	456,487

Table 5.5   Breakdown of the 'private' data in CorCenCC

Context	Genre	Location	Who	Texts	Words
private	phone_call	home	friends	2	273
			family	1	463
	conversation	—	family; spouses_and_partners	1	1163
		home	family	20	84,094
			family; parents_and_offspring	29	56,073
			family; siblings	2	14,874
			family; spouses_and_partners	22	53,202
			friends	9	25,433
			siblings	1	5221
		public_space	family; spouses_and_partners	1	864
		public_space; pub_bar_restaurant_or_cafe	family	1	2714
		school	family; parents_and_offspring	1	394
		workplace	colleagues	2	830
				92	245,598

authority areas, with the Annual Population Survey 2020 (APS) reporting Gwynedd, Cardiff, Swansea and Carmarthenshire as having the highest numbers of Welsh speakers (Welsh Government, 2020—represented by shading in the table).

In terms of Welsh proficiency, 421 contributors responded to the question 'would you describe yourself as a learner of Welsh'. Of those, 103 (24%) said 'yes' while the majority, 319 (76%), said 'no'. A similar

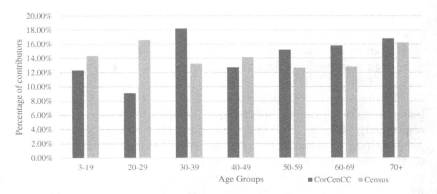

Fig. 5.1 CorCenCC's spoken demographics compared to the 2011 census (ONS, 2011)

Table 5.6 Location of spoken data contributors ($n = 515$: 298 contributors did not provide this information)

Local authority area	No	%	Local authority area	No	%
Blaenau Gwent	0	0%	Merthyr Tydfil	6	1.17%
Bridgend	11	2.14%	Monmouthshire	2	0.39%
Caerphilly	8	1.55%	Neath Port Talbot	5	0.97%
Cardiff	71	**13.79%**	Newport	2	0.39%
Carmarthenshire	75	**14.56%**	Pembrokeshire	13	2.52%
Ceredigion	15	2.91%	Powys	24	4.66%
Conwy	19	3.69%	Rest of the world	2	0.39%
Denbighshire	19	3.69%	**Rhondda Cynon Taf**	70	**13.59%**
England	2	0.39%	**Swansea**	73	**14.17%**
Flintshire	10	1.94%	Vale of Glamorgan	11	2.14%
Gwynedd	55	**10.68%**	Wrexham	9	1.75%
Isle of Anglesey	13	2.52%	—	—	—

balance of responses was provided to the question about Welsh-language ability, with **69.8%** describing themselves as fluent and **30.2%** having less developed language skills:

- I can use and understand everyday expressions and basic introductions = 2.8%

- I can communicate basic information in everyday situations = 8%
- I can communicate about familiar topics = 9.7%
- I can communicate about a wide range of topics = 9.7%
- I can communicate fluently in almost all situations = 69.8%.

Finally, in terms of occupation, 233 contributors identified as being 'employed/retired/short-term unemployed' (87% of those who responded), 28 as 'fulltime students' (10%) and six as 'never worked/long-term unemployed' (3%). 391 contributors did not respond to this question, however, which makes it difficult to provide a clear and accurate picture of the populations sampled. While these figures map well onto the original targets of 84%, 12% and 4%, this finding comes in acknowledgement of this shortcoming. As discussed in Chapter 3, while every effort should be made to collect as clear and detailed metadata when building a corpus, this is not always possible.

Also, as detailed in Chapter 3, the employment status of all individuals was further classified according to the Standard Occupation Coding scheme (SOC2010—ONS, 2010). This follows (with comparative numbers from Welsh speakers in the 2011 census detailed in '[]' below, ONS, 2011):

1. Managers, directors and senior officials: 7.6% [7.6%]
2. Professional occupations: 52.2% [19.9%]
3. Associate professional and technical occupations: 17.6% [10.6%]
4. Administrative and secretarial occupations: 8.7% [10.4%]
5. Skilled trades occupations: 9.7% [15.4%]
6. Caring, leisure and other service occupations: 0 [11.9%]
7. Sales and customer service occupations: 2.4% [7.9%]
8. Process, plant and machine operatives: 0.3% [6.1%]
9. Elementary occupations: 1.4% [10.1%].

The majority of employed contributors (who provided this metadata) are in professional occupations, which is also the largest group in the census results. The proportion of contributors in these occupations is, however, substantially higher than in the census. There is not a close mapping of contributors to the census overall, but there is evidence that individuals from a range of different employment categories contributed data.

5 RESULTS, REFLECTIONS AND LESSONS LEARNT   149

Some technical issues with the CorCenCC's Data Management Tool meant that the metadata records for the remaining questions on the speaker/author information were not fully captured, so are not discussed here. These include 'in general, how much of your communication happens in Welsh?', 'which regions of Wales have most influenced the way you speak Welsh?' and 'where did you develop your Welsh language skills?'. While this information is captured in the hard (and PDF) copies of the speaker/author information forms, there was insufficient time at the end of the project to revisit and manually extract this information from the forms.

REFLECTIONS AND LESSONS LEARNT I

The 4-million-word target for CorCenCC's spoken sub-corpus was, in retrospect, too ambitious. Notwithstanding the reduced word count, CorCenCC's spoken sub-corpus is the largest corpus of naturally occurring spoken Welsh language in existence (at over 2.86-million-words). This represents one of the main contributions of the wider CorCenCC project's work. The approach to building CorCenCC's spoken sub-corpus was principally genre/context-based, although a consideration of speaker demographics was also made. A strength of working in the Welsh-language context was that there were detailed population statistics available to inform the development of the design frame.

To replicate the approach used, it is recommended that researchers devise an initial design frame for data collection (using existing corpus design frames as a guide), including initial data collection targets for categories in the taxonomy, based on similar population data and other relevant resources. It is critical to understand, though, that this is a preliminary blueprint, and the composition of the final corpus is likely to look different to this plan. It is important not to be restricted by the design frame: if it becomes clear that a particular type of data will be difficult to obtain, it is better to take a pragmatic decision that protects time and resources, by modifying the ambition, so that other forms of easier to collect data can make up the overall shortfall.

No definitive list of spoken genres exists so by making a detailed list of possible contexts and genres (as in the design frame) only part of the picture of the language was offered. As 'spoken language exists in unknowable quantities', while an attempt can be made to create a detailed and principled design frame that attempts to capture a range of contexts

150   D. KNIGHT ET AL.

and registers, it is impossible to ever 'know how balanced or representative' a spoken corpus is (Hunston, 2002: 29). This shortcoming does not imply that the resulting corpus is not useful, simply that it is necessarily partial (and never 'perfect').

A key advantage of working with Welsh, as a minoritised language context, was that it was possible to forge close collaborations with, for example, the *Mentrau Iaith*, and organisations that promote the use of the Welsh language in each local authority of Wales. This enabled the team to reach a wide audience of Welsh speakers during participant recruitment and when publicising the project, empowering speakers to co-create a resource that was to be freely available to the public and to future generations of Welsh speakers. Throughout the project, however, issues were encountered with the under-confidence of speakers who felt that their 'colloquial' Welsh was 'incorrect' and even that '*so 'Ngwmrâg i'n ddigon da*' ('my Welsh isn't good enough'). Despite providing examples of excerpts from existing corpora, and details of how their data would (and would not) be used, offering appropriate reassurance to persuade contributors to record their own data was a challenge throughout the project. It is important to think carefully about how to access speakers; how they will be recorded across each spoken context (using more traditional to technologically advanced resources, such as CorCenCC's crowdsourcing app); how engagement with contributors will be maintained, and how conversion of their interest in the work to minutes/hours of data recorded can be maximised.

The use of the crowdsourcing app helped to increase levels of speaker motivation/engagement with Welsh-language initiatives, as well as stakeholder interest, but this did not always convert to hours/episodes recorded. In total, 298 spoken files were recorded and contributed to the project via the crowdsourcing app and/or website. While there were 187 downloads of the app, only 46 individual users contributed data. This amounted to 14 h of data, but not all this data was usable. It was often collected in noisy environments so was difficult to hear and/or transcribe or included participants for whom full consent to record was not provided. Developers of the Spoken BNC2014 commented that a reliance on modern technology 'risks excluding members of the UK population who are less familiar with computers and the associated data collection procedure, and skews the pool of speakers in the corpus in favour of the tech-savvy' (Love, 2020: 91). This is certainly a point that resonated with the team building CorCenCC. It was hoped that more data would be obtained via the app, but as the utility of crowdsourcing was already underlined to be a potential 'risk' when planning the project, plans were made to record spoken data via more traditional means as well. An additional consideration would be in ensuring that the app is available across all platforms at the same time. In the case of CorCenCC, the app was promoted when it was only available on iOS and via the web-based interface. As a result, Android users were initially unable to access the app despite having expressed an interest in engaging with it.

Potential users of the app also noted that the initial sign-up and permission process was lengthy and somewhat intimidating, often preventing them from fully engaging with the app. It was difficult to balance the need for ensuring that this approach to data collection was fully compliant to the ethical requirements alongside the need for it to be user-friendly. This challenge requires close consideration for anyone considering using a data collection app for future corpus development. To ensure that the app is maximally useful to future researchers, first, more extensive end user consultation should be carried out at each iterative stage of the interface design (to ensure that it is intuitive and that end users will be keen to use it). Second, someone with specific expertise in promoting/advertising apps should be consulted and/or employed to help to distribute it. Despite ongoing efforts to promote the app by the research team, this was perhaps not appropriately targeted to engage enough active contributors.

A further issue encountered when building the spoken sub-corpus was the availability and experience of Welsh-language transcribers. Motivated by CorCenCC's user-driven design (see Knight et al., 2021: 44–52), the project team looked directly to the Welsh-speaking community for help in this process. Transcribers received extensive training before completing work for CorCenCC, a task that should be factored into the planning phase. A team of just over 180 transcribers was recruited throughout the project. Those who transcribed regularly were initially able to produce over 400 words an hour, but this rate increased as they became more experienced transcribers and more familiar with CorCenCC's bespoke transcription conventions. Twelve of the more active transcribers were also recruited to assist with the quality control (QCing) process.

Despite providing explicit, road-tested, transcription conventions and implementing rigorous procedures to check the quality and accuracy of transcribers' work (Chapter 4), it was impossible to ensure complete consistency and accuracy of the transcriptions. While small datasets can be subjected to a process of close manual checking, this matter of quality and accuracy remains an ongoing challenge when building large-scale corpora in any language. In the development of the Spoken BNC2014, for example, it was remarked that 'it was surprising that such a variety of errors in the transcription codes could pass through quality control undetected' (Love, 2020: 169). The developers of the Spoken BNC2014 also remarked that 'in practice, it is very unlikely that a match between non-standard orthography and precise phonetic quality was achieved consistently, both within the transcripts of a given transcriber and indeed between transcribers' (Love et al., 2017: 337). This was also the case in the Welsh-language context. As transcribers were instructed to transcribe words as they heard them in a recording, a wide range of different orthographic representations of a form could potentially be captured. Efforts to mitigate this were made using the automated QCing scripts, but it is unlikely that the scripts would have captured every instance of this, particularly given the rich diversity (in terms of accent/dialect) in which Welsh is spoken.

Written Data in CorCenCC

The final composition of CorCenCC's written sub-corpus is detailed in Table 5.7 (comparing Tables 2.9–2.11 with the final corpus) and Table 5.8 (with a breakdown across genres, topics and intended audiences). This sub-corpus includes over 3.89-million-words and 704 texts. Note, again, that the tags used here are consistent with those used in the released version of the corpus, for ease of reference.

A certain level of flexibility is needed when building written corpora as, again, differences (sometimes significant) between what is initially planned and what is finally realised (i.e. the nature and amount of the data collected) are likely to occur. The first, most notable, difference between the written design frames and the final corpus composition is the changes made to the labels/taxonomy used. These changes include:

- primary, nursery and secondary prose have been combined as fiction for 'children < 11'
- nursery, primary and secondary magazines have been merged as 'children's magazines'
- some adult non-fiction genres did not exist, so were removed; new ones were added

5 RESULTS, REFLECTIONS AND LESSONS LEARNT   153

Table 5.7 Comparing CorCenCC's written sub-corpus design frame with the final sub-corpus

Genre (using categories from the original design frame, for ease of comparison)	Target		Actual	
	Words	% Of sub-corpus	Words	% Of sub-corpus
books-fiction (all audiences)	710,000	17.75%	802,260	20.6%
books-factual (inc. grammar/language/dictionaries)	780,000	19.5%	1,121,165	28.8%
song/hymns	40,000	1%	1157	>1%
Eisteddfod compositions, programmes	50,000	1.25%	0	0%
Urdd Eisteddfod compositions, programmes	50,000	1.25%	0	0%
Papurau bro	400,000	10%	117,334	3%
journals	70,000	1.75%	272,831	7%
newsletters	70,000	1.75%	78,803	2%
newspapers	50,000	1.25%	0	0%
periodicals	100,000	2.5%	0	0%
magazines (for all audiences)	80,000	2%	329,203	8.5%
letters and diaries (including formal letters)	400,000	10%	12,873	>1%
academic essays, exam scripts	200,000	5%	26,047	>1%
advertisements	100,000	2.5%	0	0%
information leaflets, political/legal documents	250,000	6.25%	792,679	20.3%
stories	400,000	10%	0	0%
signs	60,000	1.5%	3058	>1%
other	190,000	4.75%	333,705	8.6%
	4,000,000	100%	3,895,115	100%

- constituent components of the category 'grammar, language, dictionaries' are combined and relabelled 'language'
- children's 'song and hymns' merged with 'poetry' and classified as 'poetry, songs, and hymns'
- 'law, politics, education' renamed 'law and politics'
- 'recreation' renamed 'sports, leisure and lifestyle'
- 'travel, tourism' renamed 'travel and tourism'
- 'Wales, local history, local customs' renamed 'local community and history'

Table 5.8 CorCenCC's written sub-corpus composition (with revised categorisations)

Genre	Topic	Target audience	Texts	Words
academic_journal			9	272,831
book; biographies_and_autobiographies		adults	32	540,456
book-factual	educational	Welsh_learners	4	97,574
	language	adults	1	18,868
	law_and_politics	adults	2	31,872
	literature_culture_and_the_arts	adults	3	37,144
	local_community_and_history	adults	14	306,452
	music	adults	2	19,880
		children_11–18	1	3482
	religion	adults	4	31,725
	sport_leisure_and_lifestyle	adults	3	14,204
	travel_and_tourism	adults	2	19,508
book-factual; poem, song, or hymn		children_<11	3	1581
book-factual; poem, song, or hymn		adults	2	3576
book-fiction		adults	31	551,988
book-fiction		children_11–18	15	15,3772
book-fiction		children_<11	14	83,354
book-fiction		Welsh_learners	4	13,146
essays_coursework_and_exams; essay			19	23,067
essays_coursework_and_exams; exam			12	2980
leaflet_document_announcement; announcement		adults	236	112,095
leaflet_document_announcement; document		adults	65	244,261
leaflet_document_announcement; tv_listing		adults	35	429,977
leaflet_document_announcement; leaflet		adults	3	6346

Genre	Topic	Target audience	Texts	Words
Letter; template			53	12,873
magazine	literature_culture_and_the_arts	adults	74	307,988
	literature_culture_and_the_arts	children	6	21,215
miscellaneous; document			3	1636
miscellaneous; sign			1	3058
miscellaneous; diary			1	3557
newsletter		adults	33	78,803
papurau_bro	local_community_and_history	adults	13	117,334
thesis			4	328,512
			704	3,895,115

156 D. KNIGHT ET AL.

The motivation behind these changes was to:

i. make the labelling more transparent and replicable, to
ii. better reflect the language context and
iii. fully account for texts that were available.

On a practical level, relabelling was essential as there were numerous instances where it proved difficult to allocate a text to a given category. Rather than trying to make texts 'fit' a category, the categories were instead readjusted and redefined.

Nearly half (49.4%) of the written sub-corpus comprises the genre of 'books', approximately 30% of which are the genres of 'factual' (circa 586,000 words), 42% 'fiction' (circa 800,000 words) and 28% 'biographies and autobiographies' (circa 300,000 words). A range of topics is represented in the books, including 'literature, culture and the arts', 'local community and history' and 'sport, leisure and lifestyle'. While an attempt was made to achieve a certain level of balance in word count across these, it was also important to reflect:

i. the realities of the publishing industry,
ii. the availability of volumes currently in print, and
iii. what the team could legitimately gain permission to use.

Due to the constraints imposed by the relatively low numbers of Welsh books that are published annually, a certain level of flexibility with the timeframe for data collection, shifting it back a number of years (from 2015) was needed. The data collected is sampled from the following 8-year period, with the majority of the 137 books collected between 2014 and 2019 so, it remains 'contemporary':

- 2011 = 8 (5.8%)
- 2012 = 11 (8.0%)
- 2013 = 13 (9.49%)
- 2014 = 26 (19.0%)
- 2015 = 16 (11.7%)
- 2016 = 14 (10.2%)
- 2017 = 29 (21.2%)
- 2018 = 20 (14.6%)

5 RESULTS, REFLECTIONS AND LESSONS LEARNT   157

This need for flexibility in collection dates is something that was also witnessed in the creation of the Written BNC 2014 (Hawtin, 2018), among other corpora.

Academic Welsh, including academic journals (272,831 words, 7%), theses (328,512 words, 8%), essays and exams (<1%) accounts for 16% of the written sub-corpus. Collectively, these represent a higher proportion of the sub-corpus than originally planned. This was because some of these genres were initially overlooked and not accounted for in the original design frame and more journal texts became available for use than anticipated. All these texts that were made available to the team were accepted and included in the corpus. The inclusion of journal texts enables users to examine the language of this predominantly formal variety. The remaining 34% of the written corpus includes texts that Welsh speakers are likely to encounter in their daily lives. This includes leaflets, TV listings for the Welsh-language channels S4C, formal documents (from companies and school governing bodies, for example).

There was an original plan to collect 400,000 words of letters and diaries. This target was not achieved. When discussing the collection of letters for the Written BNC2014, 'it became clear that, for all of the team members, email had replaced letter writing almost entirely', so it became impossible to source this data (Hawtin, 2018: 238). This was also somewhat true in the Welsh-language context, as only very few letters, often less than 300 words each, from business contexts rather than personal communications, were successfully sourced (12,873 words). Rather than remove this category from the final corpus, however, the little that it was possible to collect was included.

Of the 602 written texts categorised according to target audience, the majority of these texts (92%) were aimed at adults, 6% at children and 1% at learners of any age.

There were 53 different individual contributors to the written data, which included 29 companies/groups of contributors. The latter of these included the publisher *Y Lolfa* (who provided books), *Gwerddon* (an academic journal) through the *Coleg Cymraeg Cenedlaethol* (academic journals), S4C (TV listings and announcements) and groups including the editor(s) who represented, for example, contributors to *papurau bro*. For these, individual speaker demographic metadata was not provided. Each text in the published corpus does, however, include metadata information regarding the publisher(s), the full publication reference and the ISBN of the text.

Of the 24 individual contributors to the written sub-corpus who *did* provide some demographic information (predominantly those who contributed, for example, theses, documents and other forms of miscellaneous material), 13 identified as female, eight male and three did not provide this information in their response. The general pattern of a higher number of female to male contributors mirrors what was seen in the spoken data. Five of the written data contributors were 60–69, four were from each of the following age groups: 20–29, 30–39, 40–49, three were aged 50–59, one was over 70 (three did not specify this information in their response). Individual contributors were predominantly located in the following local authorities: Cardiff (four people), Gwynedd (four), Newport (three) and Swansea (two). As this equates to a total of only 13 contributors, it would have been desirable to have a wider representation of contributors from areas including west Wales, north-east Wales, for example.

The majority of the written language contributors who provided their metadata were employed, retired or short-term unemployed (17), one was a full-time student and the remainder did not respond. There was not enough data provided by the contributors to undertake any assessment of the employment categories. Most contributors defined themselves as learners of Welsh, with 14 responding with 'yes' to this question and six with 'no'. This is despite the fact that the majority of respondents (13) stated that they can either 'communicate about familiar topics' or 'communicate fluently in almost all situations'. These responses do not align with the common understanding of the term 'learner'.

REFLECTIONS AND LESSONS LEARNT II

Having access to detailed statistics and information about Welsh-language books in print, and Welsh-language service providers, for example, proved invaluable when developing a comprehensive design frame for CorCenCC's 3.8-million-word written sub-corpus. While various adjustments were made between the design and the published sub-corpus, the data amassed provides a comprehensive representation of Welsh-language writing albeit with a predominance of published texts. As such, CorCenCC's written sub-corpus offers a solid foundation for examining (and comparing) texts across various genres and topics, and across all sub-corpora within the full corpus. When developing the design frame for this sub-corpus, it proved useful to not only source detailed authorship and readership information about the language context, but also to draw on the team's own experiences and understanding. Speakers of a language will likely know of specific texts/genres that can be sourced, particularly with regard to non-published and/or informal and personal texts.

While there was an aim to collect texts from a range of different publishers for CorCenCC, the majority were from just one (i.e. *Y Lolfa*, one of the project's partners). This was due to challenges faced in gaining consent for reusing materials in the corpus and because smaller Welsh-language publishers only publish a few books per year.

This challenge of consent was similarly faced, for example, when building the Written BNC2014, where in fact only one publisher gave permission to use their data, despite a range of potential publishers existing in the English-language context. The developers of the Written BNC2014 noted that 'the fact that even Cambridge University Press, who are partners on the project, could not grant us permission to include any of their texts in the corpus emphasises just how cautious publishers are regarding the commercial value of their copyrights' (Hawtin, 2018: 143). To overcome this, the Written BNC2014 team targeted open access texts for use, along with free samples available on publisher's websites, and scanned samples of texts to which the developers had legal access (Hawtin, 2018: 154). This was in line with the requirements for 'fair dealing' which is 'a legal term used to establish whether a use of copyright material is lawful or whether it infringes copyright' (*Gov.UK*, 2017).

When building the Thai National Corpus (TNC), a different consent-related challenge was encountered, insofar as it was discovered that publishers did not give permission for texts to be used and, instead, authors had to provide permission directly (Aroonmanakun et al., 2009). This made the process of obtaining permission a complex and time-consuming one. An alternative approach was attempted when building the first iteration of the American National Corpus (ANC), whereby only texts that were not protected by copyright were sought for inclusion. This led to only a few texts being available for the ANC and is a contributing factor as to why the original plans for this corpus never fully came to fruition (Ide, 2008). Approaches to consent, permissions and the reusability of published texts are not necessarily uniform, so understanding and identifying what is permissible within your own language context is critical. An interesting finding about the Welsh-language context was that although the majority of published texts came from one publisher, this publisher granted permission for *an expansive amount* of their texts to be used. This may (or may not) be the same in other minoritised language contexts (although the availability/scale of what is on hand is likely to be smaller than in major language contexts).

Although the final composition of the corpus shares some similarities with the initial design frame in Tables 2.1–2.11, there have been many changes to:

    i. the labels of specific categories within the corpus, and
    ii. the distribution of word counts across specific genres.

These changes were required to achieve the targets set. Throughout the project, progress towards the initial targets was closely monitored and adjusted as required. In many instances, specific targets had the potential to be reduced by up to 10%, and others were increased. While particular attention was given to ensuring that CorCenCC's design reflected current social, cultural, geographical elements bearing upon contemporary Welsh as well as the domains in which it is used, principled opportunism played an important role too. Developers of the SCOTS corpus noted that 'opportunism, although often a necessary evil, is not necessarily indefensible so long as the collection method itself is transparent' (Douglas, 2003: 34). It is important to revisit and revise targets for data collection regularly as work progresses, and to be flexible and responsive to the need to change, but also to provide clear accounts of/justifications for any changes made.

E-Language Data in CorCenCC

Table 5.9 details the composition of CorCenCC's final sub-corpus: e-language. As explained above, the target for this sub-corpus doubled from 2-million-words to 4-million-words during the project. Collectively, the blog and website texts comprise nearly 95% of the sub-corpus (i.e. significantly higher than originally targeted/anticipated), with email and SMS at 5% (i.e. significantly lower than originally targeted/anticipated). The sub-corpus extends to over 4.4-million-words and includes 9397 texts from a total of 159 different contributors (across all genres).s

Note, again, that the specific tags used in this table, and Table 5.10, are consistent with those used in the released CorCenCC dataset (v1.0.0), for ease of reference. The smallest e-language genre, in terms of word count,

5 RESULTS, REFLECTIONS AND LESSONS LEARNT   161

Table 5.9 Composition of the e-language sub-corpus in CorCenCC

Genre	Context	Target % of sub-corpus	Actual		
			Texts	Words	% Of sub-corpus
blog		30%	48	2,345,909	53.3%
website		30%	81	1,820,999	41.4%
email	professional	20%	67	10,690	3.2%
	private		215	13,404	
email_mailing_list			499	117,460	
SMS	private	20%	887	93,541	2.1%
		100%	9397	4,402,003	100%

Table 5.10 Website and blog topics of CorCenCC's e-language sub-corpus

Topic (context in italics)	Blogs		Websites	
	Texts	Words	Texts	Words
business and finance	0	0	3	129,841
food, drink and cookery	2	86,160	2	280,182
health and well-being	0	0	3	120,309
hobbies and pastimes	2	93,860	2	8050
language	3	157,286	6	85,324
law and politics	5	341,795	5	372,910
literature, culture, and the arts	10	425,285	5	49,237
local community and history	6	399,548	5	131,291
music	2	81,779	7	22,634
news, media and current affairs	3	76,593	1	175,976
personal and daily life	6	220,222	0	0
religion	1	29,366	8	103,775
teaching, academia and education	1	33,550	8	187,325
technology, computers and gaming	3	138,146	2	35,163
travel and tourism	2	164,298	4	22,715
weather, the environment and agriculture	2	98,021	0	0
TV programmes and films	0	0	2	32,174
retail and services	0	0	18	64,093
	48	2,345,909	81	1,820,999

is that of SMS. The team managed to collect an impressive 8487 texts but, given that their average length is relatively short, this amounted to just under 100,000 words. The second smallest genre is emails, with a total of just over 140k words. The topics covered by the website and blog texts are detailed in Table 5.10.

The data here is classified according to 17 'topics' (i.e. websites/blogs *about* something) and one 'context' (i.e. *retail and services*—websites that *are* something, that is, performing a specific function). While many of the broad topics from CANELC's classification scheme are seen here, these have been realigned and renamed to better fit the Welsh-language context and to offer some consistency in the labelling of texts across the different modes of data (i.e. enabling users to, for example, compare e-language texts with the topic of 'literature, culture and the arts' with written texts of the same topic).

Most of the topic categories in this sub-corpus contain at least 100,000 words, many with over 200,000 words. 'Law and politics', 'local history and community' and 'literature, culture and the arts' are the most densely populated topics across the blogs and websites, amounting to over 714,530 and 474,000 words, respectively.

It is also noted that there is a high level of variability in text length here (across the individual texts). As discussed in Chapter 2, the optimum sample size for written and e-language was 15,000 words. However some flexibility with this target was often required, and a 'full text' approach was needed for some e-language sources, where specific genres of texts were difficult to collect. Despite extensive marketing and recruitment campaigns, it proved difficult to obtain full informed consent from an extensive range of contributors to the e-language data. This led to the use of a more opportunistic and pragmatic approach to data collection, with fewer sources sampled, and a larger number of words taken from each.

Of the 159 contributors to the e-language sub-corpus, 111 were companies (who provided no demographic information) and 48 were individuals. Of the individuals, 26 were female, 16 male and six individuals provided no response. The predominance of female contributors mirrors the basic patterns also seen in the spoken and written sub-corpora. The ages of these contributors are detailed below (with the percentage of those who responded detailed in parentheses):

- Up to 19 = 0
- 20–29 = 15 (31.3%)
- 30–39 = 8 (16.7%)
- 40–49 = 4 (8.3%)
- 50–59 = 7 (14.6%)
- 60–69 = 6 (12.5%)
- 70+ = 2 (4.2%)
- No response = 6

While there were contributors in all age groups (aside from the under 20s), the total number across all groups, and each group, is relatively small throughout. Of these contributors, the majority, 67% (32), of respondents described their employment status as 'employed/retired/short-term unemployed', of which most were employed in 'professional occupations' (13) and 'associate professional and technical occupations' (five), with some as 'managers, directors and senior officials' (three) and 'sales and customer service occupations' (one). The remaining contributors provided no response to this question (10).

Only 44 e-language contributors provided details of their location. The majority of these were based in Cardiff (18), followed by Swansea and Gwynedd (seven each).

Finally, 45 contributors responded to the question 'would you describe yourself as a learner of Welsh'. Most of these respondents, 80% (35), responded 'no' and 20% (eight) responded 'yes'. In total, 44 of these individuals answered the follow-up question about their use of Welsh, with the responses detailed below (with the percentage of those who responded detailed in parentheses):

- I can communicate about a wide range of topics = 3 (6.7%)
- I can communicate about familiar topics = 1 (2.2%)
- I can communicate fluently in almost all situations = 37 (82.2%)
- I can use and understand everyday expressions and basic introductions = 3 (6.7%)
- No response = 4.

These responses provide a similar pattern to those who contributed spoken data to the corpus, with the highest proportion of contributors responding with 'I can communicate fluently in almost all situations'.

REFLECTIONS AND LESSONS LEARNT III

Extending to over 4.4-million-words of data, the genres covered by CorCenCC's e-language texts enable the useful comparison of this sub-corpus within/across different modes, helping users to characterise the impact technology has on, for example, levels of formality in a text and general patterns of digital language use. This sub-corpus adds to the e-language corpora that already exist in Welsh. While a bespoke web-scraper was created (Chapter 3) to assist with the collection of e-language texts, there are a number of these tools being built to support data collection (and management) in different languages (Chapter 1). It is therefore useful to examine, in detail, what is available, both in terms of genres/texts (consent permitting) but also the utilities to extract data. There is no need to reinvent the wheel.

Given that Welsh is used extensively online, it was possible to replicate the approaches to the collection and codification of e-language data from a major language context (via CANELC)—this is something that other minoritised language contexts might also achieve. It does not go to say that CorCenCC's e-language sub-corpus is 'perfect', however. As with any other corpus, there are facets that would benefit from improvement into the future, including achieving:

- a greater number, and better balance, of topics and text genres
- a greater range of contributors to specific text genres (including blogs and websites)
- more detailed/complete metadata information to be collected from contributors to e-language texts, and
- a greater range of texts and/or topics covered (with a lower amount of data from each).

Since CorCenCC was launched (November 2020), Twitter, for example, have modified their 'rules of the road' to enable greater flexibility in the access to, and use of, their data for academic research (Twitter, 2021). This ever-changing landscape suggests that in the future

5 RESULTS, REFLECTIONS AND LESSONS LEARNT 165

it might be possible to include a wider range of e-language genres, including social media texts. It is, again, vital for those embarking on their own corpus building project(s) to find out about what is legal and considered ethically acceptable regarding the reuse of e-data in your own context (and at the time relevant to the composition of your dataset).

While steps were taken to achieve the targets listed in the design frame in Table 2.11, it was not possible to fully achieve these within the lifespan of the project. This was due to a range of factors. First, when dealing with, for example, SMS texts, 'privacy is a major concern, as the majority of phone owners are uncomfortable with having their private messages revealed, even when the purpose is for research and academic pursuits' (Chen & Kan, 2011: 301). As with emails, it was difficult to persuade Welsh speakers to share their SMSs. When inviting people to contribute their e-data to the corpus, researchers on the project were again often faced by the following response: *So 'Ngwmrâg i'n ddigon da* (My Welsh isn't good enough). At local engagement events, participants often emphasised the importance of ensuring their dialect and its lexicon be included in CorCenCC yet avoided contributing data because they self-evaluated as having poor levels of Welsh. This was something that was particularly relevant to the collection of spoken data (as discussed above) but was equally apparent for more personal forms of e-language including SMS and emails. The more personal the data, the more contributors felt exposed to this issue (despite extensive reassurance being given about this).

Second, while a number of individuals initially responded with enthusiasm to contributing data, obtaining full permission from them, with the completion of the consent and speaker/author information forms, proved challenging. Individuals often simply did not respond to follow-up emails requesting the completion of these forms. This was possibly due to the length of the forms and the time they took to complete or, as fed back informally from one contributor, their formal nature, making the process of contributing slightly intimidating (again, somewhat aligning to *So 'Ngwmrâg i'n ddigon da*). This led to a mid-project change in approach in obtaining consent, with permission sought by participants explicitly granting consent to use the data in the corpus via email. While this change led to increased success in the converting of contributor interest/enthusiasm to the permissible collection of data, it was sometimes to the detriment of obtaining full speaker/author information (as follow-up correspondence(s) that requested such additional information were often ignored/not answered). Given this, it is advisable to be prepared to revisit and revise approaches to gaining consent depending on what is permissible and/or relevant to your own research context.

In future iterations of the corpus, and in the production of similar corpora in other language contexts, a greater emphasis on further awareness raising of the project and more extensive recruitment of potential contributors is desirable. Where possible, seek (and/or pay for) advice from individuals with the appropriate expertise to facilitate this. Where the number of speakers of a language is a lot smaller than in major language contexts, a higher proportion of the speakers inevitably need to be engaged and willing to contribute data. This holds true for the spoken and written sub-corpora as well.

Concluding Remarks

This book has provided a detailed and practical account of how the CorCenCC corpus was built, with indications of how the approach used might be adapted for other language contexts. The published CorCenCC corpus (v1.0.0) extends to over 11.2-million-words, across the three modes detailed above (i.e. spoken, written, e-language). The data included in CorCenCC acts as a snapshot of the Welsh language as it was used in 2015–2020.

CorCenCC's full dataset, and the digital infrastructure created to build/host the corpus (which may be adapted for use in any language), are publicly available under the Creative Commons CC-BY-SA v4 licence (see www.corcencc.org/download). The corpus can be analysed online using CorCenCC's bespoke query tools (that are integrated with the dataset—see Chapter 4). Alternatively, existing corpus analysis tools can be used to analyse the dataset (e.g. AntConc—Anthony, 2020; WMatrix—Rayson, 2002; CQPWeb—Hardie, 2012 and #LancsBox—Brezina et al., 2020), although it should be noted that not all functionalities in these tools are fully compatible with the characters used in Welsh (e.g. $\hat{W}/\hat{w}$ and $\hat{Y}/\hat{y}$). It is advisable to check the compatibility of these tools with any unique elements that your own language corpus may possess if you plan to use these to query your own dataset.

As a national corpus, CorCenCC enables users to ask a range of questions about the use of Welsh. Some of the questions that could be explored include:

- Which genres of written language are closest to spoken and/or e-language ones? How can the patterns observed contribute to an informed debate on how 'standard' forms of a language might look in the future?
- What specific patterns can be identified as being characteristic of more formal versus informal genres/contexts/topics of language use? Where do, for example, specific genres of e-language (as opposed to spoken and/or written language) fit in a formal-informal language continuum?
- How does language use vary intergenerationally and socio-demographically? Are specific lexical items and/or grammatical structures more likely to be used by speakers of a certain age and/or socio-demographic profile?
- What neologisms can be identified in the language? Are these characteristics of, for example, particular modes or genres of the language? What evidence is there for how these were brought into the language and how borrowings became embedded in the lexicon?
- What does a spoken sub-corpus tell us about the continued vibrancy of traditional geographical dialects? Can 'new' emerging dialects be found and how might these be defined?

These kinds of questions provide a useful starting point for analysing a national corpus in any language.

A corpus that is principled in its design, aiming to represent the diversity of contemporary speakers and to reflect the wide range of contexts in which they use the language, is well positioned to provide evidence-based responses to questions of this nature. In the particular (although not exclusive) context of an under-resourced/minoritised language, corpus builders need to understand that while some of the responses to these questions will be welcomed by their language community, other responses may be a source of disagreement and/or be resisted/debated. This is because the evidence presented by corpora (based on *actual* usage) may be at odds with how members of a language community intuitively *think* a language is, or *ought* to be, used. Informing such debate is an important contribution of a corpus as it prompts the wider language community to

168   D. KNIGHT ET AL.

reflect on and discuss their own language use on the basis of real-life data rather than subjective assumptions. Being able to make language planning and policy decisions based on robust evidence is a valuable step in helping to maintain the health and vitality of a language context and community, serving to underline just some of the impact that a resource such as a national corpus in any language can have.

REFERENCES

Anthony, L. (2020). *AntConc (Version 3.5.9)* [Software]. Waseda University. Retrieved from https://www.laurenceanthony.net/software [Accessed 20/06/2021].

Aroonmanakun, W., Tansiri, K., & Nittayanuparp, P. (2009). Thai national corpus: A progress report. In *Proceedings of the 7th Workshop on Asian Language Resources (ALR7)* (pp. 153–158). Suntec, Singapore.

Brezina, V., Weill-Tessier, P., & McEnery, A. (2020). *#LancsBox v. 5.x*. [Software]. Lancaster University. Retrieved from http://corpora.lancs.ac.uk/lancsbox [Accessed 20/06/2021].

Chen, T., & Kan, M.-Y. (2011). Creating a live, public short message service corpus: The NUS SMS corpus. *Language Resources and Evaluation, 47*, 299–335.

Douglas, F. (2003). The Scottish corpus of texts and speech: Problems of corpus design. *Literary and Linguistic Computing, 18*, 23–37.

Gov.UK. (2017). *Intellectual property—Guidance. Exceptions to copyright.* Retrieved from https://www.gov.uk/exceptions-to-copyright [Accessed 20/06/2021].

Hardie, A. (2012). CQPweb—Combining power, flexibility and usability in a corpus analysis tool. *International Journal of Corpus Linguistics, 17*, 380–409.

Hawtin, A. (2018). *The written British national corpus 2014: Design, compilation and analysis.* Unpublished Ph.D. thesis, Lancaster University.

Hunston, S. (2002). *Corpora in applied linguistics.* Cambridge University Press.

Ide, N. (2008). The American national corpus: Then, now, and tomorrow. *Selected Proceedings of the 2008 HCSNet Workshop on Designing the Australian National Corpus: Mustering Languages* (pp. 108–113). Sommerville, MA.

Knight, D., Morris, S., & Fitzpatrick, T. (2021). *Corpus design and construction in minoritised language contexts: The national corpus of contemporary Welsh.* Palgrave.

Love, R. (2020). *Overcoming challenges in corpus construction.* Routledge.

Love, R., Dembry, C., Hardie, A., Brezina, V., & McEnery, T. (2017). The spoken BNC2014: Designing and building a spoken corpus of everyday conversations. *International Journal of Corpus Linguistics, 22*, 319–344.

ONS (Office for National Statistics). (2010). *SOC2010 volume 1: Structure and descriptions of unit groups*. Retrieved from https://www.ons.gov.uk/met hodology/classificationsandstandards/standardoccupationalclassificationsoc/ soc2010/soc2010volume1structureanddescriptionsofunitgroups#summar ising-changes-to-the-classification-structure-introduced-in-soc2010 [Accessed 20/06/2021].

ONS (Office for National Statistics). (2011). *Census: Digitised boundary data (England and Wales)* [Computer File]. Retrieved from https://borders.ukd ataservice.ac.uk/ [Accessed 20/06/2021].

Rayson, P. (2002). *Matrix: A statistical method and software tool for linguistic analysis through corpus comparison*. Unpublished PhD thesis, Lancaster University.

Twitter. (2021). *Twitter rules and policies* [Online]. Retrieved from https://help. twitter.com/en/rules-and-policies#twitter-rules [Accessed 20/06/2021].

Welsh Government. (2020). *Annual population survey (APS): July 2019 to June 2020*. Cardiff. Retrieved from https://gov.wales/annual-population-survey-july-2019-june-2020 [Accessed 20/06/2021].

APPENDICES

Appendix 1: Recording Notice

Heddiw, rydym yn recordio ar gyfer Corpws Cenedlaethol Cymraeg Cyfoes

We are recording today for the National Corpus of Contemporary Welsh

Os byddai'n well gennych beidio â chael eich recordio, rhowch wybod wrth gyrraedd y man talu

If you would prefer not to be recorded, please tell us as you approach the till

Bydd y data sy'n cael eu casglu yu cael eu trawsgrifio, eu gwneud yn ddi-enw a'u hychwanegu at y corpws (casgliad arlein o'r Gymraeg) er lles dysgwyr, ymchwilwyr a chyhoeddwyr ayb y dyfodol.

Data collected will be transcribed and anonymised and added to the corpus (an online collection of the Welsh language) for the benefit of future learners, researchers and publishers etc.

© The Editor(s) (if applicable) and The Author(s), under exclusive licence to Springer Nature Switzerland AG 2021
D. Knight et al., *Building a National Corpus*,
https://doi.org/10.1007/978-3-030-81858-6

172 APPENDICES

Appendix 2: Post-Recording Information Sheet

Taflen wybodaeth

Diolch yn fawr iawn am gytuno i gael eich recordio heddiw ar gyfer prosiect CorCenCC. Prosiect ymchwil cydweithredol yw hwn sy'n cael ei arwain gan Brifysgol Caerdydd (gyda Phrifysgolion Abertawe, Bangor a Chaerhirfryn) â'r nod o adeiladu **CorCenCC: Corpws Cenedlaethol Cymraeg Cyfoes**. Casgliad o ddata iaith lafar, ysgrifenedig a digidol yw corpws sy'n gallu helpu rhoi ciplun o iaith fel y mae'n cael ei defnyddio mewn gwirionedd. Y bwriad yw bod corpws CorCenCC ar gael yn rhwydd ar-lein ar sail ffynhonnell agored fel cronfa ddata gyfrifiadurol chwiliadwy i unrhyw un sy'n dymuno ei ddefnyddio.

Ceir rhagor o wybodaeth am y prosiect ar wefan CorCenCC: http://sites.cardiff.ac.uk/corcencc/cy

Ceir gwybodaeth lawn ynghylch sut bydd Prifysgol Caerdydd yn prosesu ac yn defnyddio'r recordiadau yma: http://app.corcencc.org/consent/mobile/cy. Os byddwch chi'n newid eich meddwl ynglŷn â chaniatáu i recordiadau sy'n eich cynnwys chi gael eu defnyddio ar gyfer prosiect CorCenCC, cysylltwch â CorCenCC@caerdydd.ac.uk, gan roi enw'r siop/cwmni/sefydliad lle y cawsoch eich recordio, dyddiad y recordio, ac amser y recordio (os yn bosibl).

Os oes gennych chi unrhyw gwestiynau, ymholiadau neu broblemau am hyn, cysylltwch â: CorCenCC@caerdydd.ac.uk.

APPENDICES 173

Information sheet

Thank you very much for agreeing to be recorded today for the CorCenCC project. This collaborative research project led by Cardiff University (with Swansea, Bangor and Lancaster Universities) aims to build **CorCenCC: The National Corpus of Contemporary Welsh**. A corpus is a collection of spoken, written and digital language data that can help provide a snapshot of language as it is used in 'real-life' situations. The intention is for the CorCenCC corpus to be made freely available online on an open-source basis as a searchable computerised database to anyone wishing to have access to it.

More information about the project can be found on the CorCenCC website: http://sites.cardiff.ac.uk/corcencc

Full information about how Cardiff University will process and use the recordings can be found here: http://app.corcencc.org/consent/mobile. If you change your mind about allowing recordings which feature you to be used for the CorCenCC project, contact CorCenCC@cardiff.ac.uk, giving the name of the shop/company/establishment where you were recorded, the date of the recording, and the time of the recording (if possible).

If you have any questions, queries or problems about any of this, please contact: CorCenCC@cardiff.ac.uk.

Appendix 3: App Recruitment Information

What is a corpus?

Essentially, a corpus is a **bank of words**, but a corpus is not the same as a dictionary. When a user searches for a word in a corpus, they are able to see many **examples of the words in their original contexts**, as they were used by the original authors or speakers. Users can also find out, for instance, how frequently a specific word is used, or create quizzes to **help with language learning**. In a nutshell, a corpus is a valuable electronic tool which allows us to **better understand our language**.

Building the National Corpus of Contemporary Welsh

In order to create this resource, we are collecting examples of spoken, written and digital Welsh from people of all ages and from every corner of Wales. We aim to collect 10 million words in total – and so we need your help! We want your Welsh!

CorCenCC Crowdsourcing App

The CorCenCC crowdsourcing app – now available on iOS, Android and via the web – allows Welsh speakers to record their conversations across a range of contexts. **In which contexts do you use Welsh?** At home, at work, whilst socialising with friends? You can record anywhere you want! And nobody will know who you are so no need to worry about that either!

The app makes contributing to the corpus **really easy**, and it will allow us to include data that is as **natural** and as representative of **everyday Welsh** as possible.

The app is free to use and you can download it via the App Store (iOS) or Google Play (Android), or you can contribute by going to: http://app.corcencc.org

Beth yw corpws?

Yn y bôn, **banc o eiriau** yw corpws, ond dyw corpws ddim yr un fath â geiriadur. Pan fydd defnyddwyr yn chwilio am air mewn corpws, byddan nhw'n gallu gweld llawer o **enghreifftiau o'r geiriau yn eu cyd-destunau gwreiddiol**, fel eu bod wedi cael eu defnyddio gan yr awduron neu'r siaradwyr gwreiddiol. Gall defnyddwyr hefyd gael gwybod, er enghraifft, pa mor aml y mae gair penodol yn cael ei ddefnyddio, neu greu cwisiau i **helpu gyda dysgu ieithoedd**. Yn gryno, mae corpws yn offeryn electronig gwerthfawr sy'n caniatáu i ni **ddeall ein hiaith yn well**.

Adeiladu Corpws Cenedlaethol Cymraeg Cyfoes

Er mwyn creu'r adnodd hwn, rydyn ni'n casglu enghreifftiau o Gymraeg llafar, ysgrifenedig a digidol gan bobl o bob oedran ac o bob cwr o Gymru. Rydyn ni'n anelu at gasglu 10 miliwn o eiriau mewn cyfanswm – ac felly rydyn ni angen eich help! Rhowch eich Cymraeg i ni!

Corpws Cenedlaethol Cymraeg Cyfoes
National Corpus of Contemporary Welsh

Ap Torfoli CorCenCC

Mae ap torfoli CorCenCC – sydd bellach ar gael ar iOS, Android a thrwy'r we – yn caniatáu i siaradwyr Cymraeg recordio eu sgyrsiau ar draws ystod o gyd-destunau. **Ym mha gyd-destunau dych chi'n defnyddio'r Gymraeg?** Gartre, yn y gwaith, wrth gymdeithasu gyda ffrindiau? Cewch chi recordio unrhyw le dych chi eisiau! A fydd neb yn gwybod pwy ydych chi, felly does dim rhaid poeni am hynny chwaith!

Mae'r ap yn gwneud y broses o gyfrannu at y corpws yn **hawdd iawn**, ac mae'n caniatáu i ni gynnwys iaith yn y corpws sydd mor **naturiol** â phosib ac sy'n adlewyrchu **iaith bob dydd** siaradwyr Cymraeg.

Mae'r ap yn rhad ac am ddim a gallwch ei lawrlwytho drwy'r App Store (iOS) neu Google Play (Android), neu gallwch gyfrannu drwy fynd i: http://app.corcencc.org

 www.facebook.com/CorCenCC   https://twitter.com/corcencc   www.corcencc.cymru/ap

Appendix 4: Speaker/Author Information Form

Corpws Cenedlaethol Cymraeg Cyfoes
National Corpus of Contemporary Welsh

Speaker/Author Information Form
In order for us to ensure that the corpus content reflects the language of all users of Welsh, please answer the questions below.

First name	Year of birth
Surname	

Gender
Female   Male   Other   Prefer not to say

Where do you live?

☐ Blaenau Gwent	☐ Gwynedd	☐ Swansea
☐ Bridgend	☐ Isle of Anglesey	☐ Torfaen
☐ Caerphilly	☐ Merthyr Tydfil	☐ Vale of Glamorgan
☐ Cardiff	☐ Monmouthshire	☐ Wrexham
☐ Carmarthenshire	☐ Neath Port Talbot	---------------
☐ Ceredigion	☐ Newport	☐ England
☐ Conwy	☐ Pembrokeshire	☐ Northern Ireland
☐ Denbighshire	☐ Powys	☐ Scotland
☐ Flintshire	☐ Rhondda Cynon Taff	☐ Rest of the world

Occupation
☐ Full-time student
☐ Never worked / Long-term unemployed
☐ Employed / Retired / Short-term unemployed

If you are employed, retired, or short-term unemployed, what is/was the full title of your main job?

In general, how much of your communication happens in Welsh?

☐ Up to 24% ☐ 25-49% ☐ 50-74% ☐ 75%+

Which regions of Wales have most influenced the way you speak Welsh? (Tick as many as apply)

☐ North West ☐ South West
☐ North East ☐ South East
☐ Mid Wales ☐ Other (please give details)

_____

Where did you develop your Welsh language skills? (Tick as many as apply)

☐ At home and/or with my family, as a child
☐ Welsh-medium nursery
☐ Welsh-medium/bilingual primary school
☐ English-medium primary school
☐ Welsh-medium/bilingual secondary school
☐ English-medium secondary school
☐ College

☐ University
☐ Welsh for Adults course
☐ Self-study
☐ Informal contact with Welsh as an adult
☐ Informal contact with Welsh as a child
☐ Other (please give details)

_____

How would you describe your ability in Welsh?
☐ I can communicate fluently in almost all situations.
☐ I can communicate about a wide range of topics.
☐ I can communicate about familiar topics.
☐ I can communicate basic information in everyday situations.
☐ I can use and understand everyday expressions and basic introductions.

Would you describe yourself as a learner of Welsh?
☐ Yes
☐ No

If you have ticked 'Yes', please state the level of your most recent Welsh course:

_____

If you would like us to add you to the project email list, to keep you updated on CorCenCC news and developments, please tick here: ☐

Email address:

_____

APPENDICES

Corpws Cenedlaethol Cymraeg Cyfoes
National Corpus of Contemporary Welsh

Ffurflen Wybodaeth yr Awdur/Siaradwr
Er mwyn i ni sicrhau bod cynnwys y corpws yn adlewyrchu iaith pawb sy'n defnyddio'r Gymraeg, atebwch y cwestiynau isod, os gwelwch yn dda.

Enw cyntaf	Blwyddyn geni
Cyfenw	
Rhyw Benyw Gwryw Arall	Gwell gennyf beidio â dweud
Ble rydych chi'n byw? ☐ Abertawe ☐ Blaenau Gwent ☐ Bro Morgannwg ☐ Caerdydd ☐ Caerffili ☐ Casnewydd ☐ Castell-nedd Port Talbot ☐ Ceredigion ☐ Conwy	☐ Gwynedd ☐ Sir y Fflint ☐ Merthyr Tudful ☐ Torfaen ☐ Pen-y-bont ar Ogwr ☐ Wrecsam ☐ Powys ☐ Ynys Môn ☐ Rhondda Cynon Taf ☐ -------------- ☐ Sir Benfro ☐ Gogledd Iwerddon ☐ Sir Ddinbych ☐ Lloegr ☐ Sir Fynwy ☐ Yr Alban ☐ Sir Gaerfyrddin ☐ Gweddill y byd
Galwedigaeth ☐ Myfyriwr llawn-amser ☐ Erioed wedi gweithio / Yn ddi-waith tymor hir ☐ Cyflogedig / Wedi ymddeol / Yn ddi-waith tymor byr **Os ydych chi'n gyflogedig, wedi ymddeol, neu'n ddi-waith tymor byr, beth yw/oedd teitl llawn eich prif swydd?**	

APPENDICES 179

Yn gyffredinol, faint o'ch cyfathrebu sy'n digwydd trwy'r Gymraeg?

☐ Hyd at 24%   ☐ 25-49%   ☐ 50-74%   ☐ 75%+

Pa rannau o Gymru sydd wedi dylanwadu fwyaf ar y ffordd rydych chi'n siarad Cymraeg? (Ticiwch bob un sy'n berthnasol)

☐ Gogledd-orllewin   ☐ De-orllewin
☐ Gogledd-ddwyrain   ☐ De-ddwyrain
☐ Canolbarth   ☐ Arall (rhowch fanylion

_____

Ble rydych chi wedi meithrin eich sgiliau Cymraeg? (Ticiwch bob un sy'n berthnasol)

☐ Yn y cartref a/neu gyda fy nheulu, fel plentyn   ☐ Prifysgol
☐ Meithrinfa cyfrwng Cymraeg   ☐ Cwrs Cymraeg i Oedolion
☐ Ysgol gynradd cyfrwng Cymraeg/ddwyieithog   ☐ Hunan-astudio
☐ Ysgol gynradd cyfrwng Saesneg   ☐ Cyswllt anffurfiol â'r Gymraeg fel oedolyn
☐ Ysgol uwchradd cyfrwng Cymraeg/ddwyieithog   ☐ Cyswllt anffurfiol â'r Gymraeg fel plentyn
☐ Ysgol uwchradd cyfrwng Saesneg   ☐ Arall (rhowch fanylion)
☐ Coleg   _____

Sut byddech chi'n disgrifio'ch gallu yn y Gymraeg?

☐ Rwy'n gallu cyfathrebu'n rhugl ym mron pob sefyllfa.
☐ Rwy'n gallu cyfathrebu am ystod eang o bynciau.
☐ Rwy'n gallu cyfathrebu am bynciau cyfarwydd.
☐ Rwy'n gallu cyfathrebu gwybodaeth sylfaenol mewn sefyllfaoedd pob dydd.
☐ Rwy'n gallu defnyddio a deall ymadroddion pob dydd a chyflwyniadau sylfaenol.

Fyddech chi'n disgrifio'ch hunan fel dysgwr/dysgwraig Cymraeg?

☐ Byddwn
☐ Na fyddwn

Os ydych chi wedi ticio 'Byddwn', nodwch lefel eich cwrs Cymraeg diweddaraf:

_____

Os ydych chi eisiau cael eich rhoi ar restr e-bost y prosiect, er mwyn i ni anfon y newyddion a'r datblygiadau diweddaraf am CorCenCC atoch chi, ticiwch yma: ☐

Cyfeiriad e-bost:

_____

Appendix 5: Transcriber Recruitment Information

A fyddai gennych chi ddiddordeb mewn gweithio fel trawsgrifydd ar gyfer CorCenCC?

Fel y gwyddoch, rydyn ni wedi bod yn brysur yn recordio pobl yn siarad Cymraeg ledled y wlad. Mae'r gwaith trawsgrifio'r recordiadau wedi dechrau, ond rydyn ni bellach yn chwilio am ragor o drawsgrifwyr – **a fyddai gennych chi ddiddordeb?**

Mae'r gwaith yn hyblyg (cewch weithio pryd bynnag sy'n eich siwtio chi, a gwneud cymaint/cyn lleied o oriau a fynnwch chi) felly mae'n hawdd ei ffitio o gwmpas gweithgareddau eraill, ac mae'r recordiadau yn ddiddorol ac yn amrywiol – un diwrnod efallai byddwch chi'n trawsgrifio darlith neu bregeth, a'r diwrnod nesaf sgwrs fywiog lawr yn y dafarn!

Pe byddai gennych chi ddiddordeb mewn ymuno â'n tîm o drawsgrifwyr, ebostiwch trawsgrifio@corcencc.org am ragor o wybodaeth, os gwelwch yn dda.

Would you be interested in working as a CorCenCC transcriber?

As you know, we have been busy recording Welsh being spoken up and down the country. Work has begun on transcribing the recordings, but we are now looking for more transcribers – **would you be interested?**

The work is flexible (you can work whenever suits you, and do as many/few hours as you wish) so it is easy to fit in around other activities, and the recordings are interesting and varied – one day you might be transcribing a lecture or sermon, and the next day a lively conversation down the pub!

If you'd be interested in joining our team of transcribers, please email trawsgrifio@corcencc.org for more information.

www.facebook.com/CorCenCC   https://twitter.com/corcencc   www.corcencc.cymru/ap

INDEX

A

access/accessibility, 8–10, 15, 38, 47, 48, 65, 77, 79, 121, 131, 150, 151, 158, 159, 164

anonymisation, 4, 97, 98, 113–117

B

balance, 11, 24, 25, 30, 33, 49, 63–65, 139, 147, 151, 156, 164

C

Cambridge and Nottingham e-Language Corpus (CANELC), 60–62, 64, 66, 162, 164

categorisation, 27, 47, 60, 61, 66, 86

coding scheme, 60, 62

context, vi, 2, 4–11, 14, 16–18, 24, 26–49, 53, 56, 61, 63–66, 68, 79, 83, 87, 89, 91, 92, 95, 99, 112, 116, 118, 119, 124, 129, 130, 138–143, 146, 149, 150, 152, 156, 157, 159–162, 164–168

copyright, 28, 48, 95, 159

corpus manager(s), 120

crowdsourcing, 61, 79, 82, 83, 121, 150, 151

D

data collection, 5, 11, 25, 27, 35, 40, 44, 61, 63, 68, 78, 81–83, 85, 96, 97, 138, 149–151, 156, 160, 162, 164

data management (tool), 86, 120, 122, 123, 149

demographic, 11, 16, 17, 29, 30, 32, 36, 46, 53, 63, 85, 87, 92, 95, 143, 147, 149, 157, 158, 162

design frame, 3, 4, 11, 18, 25–28, 30, 32, 33, 36–43, 45–47, 49, 50, 52–55, 59, 60, 62, 63, 65–68, 75, 81, 92, 121, 137, 143, 149, 152, 153, 157, 158, 160, 165

dialect, 55, 78, 83, 85–89, 96, 110, 152, 165

© The Editor(s) (if applicable) and The Author(s), under exclusive licence to Springer Nature Switzerland AG 2021
D. Knight et al., *Building a National Corpus*,
https://doi.org/10.1007/978-3-030-81858-6

182 INDEX

E
e-language (corpora), 58, 59, 62, 164

G
genre, 2, 6, 7, 11, 12, 16, 24, 25, 27–33, 36–49, 52, 53, 55–57, 59–64, 66, 67, 91, 92, 120, 124, 129, 130, 139–146, 149, 152–156, 158–162, 164, 165
good practice, 98

L
lesser-used language, vi, 2

M
major/majority language, 4, 5, 7, 8, 11, 36, 48, 66, 79, 96, 118, 160, 164, 166
metadata, 6, 13, 16, 49, 62, 75, 83–85, 87, 89, 91, 92, 94, 95, 97, 120, 121, 124, 126, 148, 149, 157, 158, 164
minoritised (language(s)), vi, 4, 7–10, 14, 18, 56, 66, 107, 118, 150, 160, 164, 167
minority (language(s)), vi, 7–9, 11, 66, 116
mode(s), 2, 3, 7, 16, 25–28, 55, 56, 59, 63, 68, 95, 114, 116, 120, 123, 124, 126, 127, 129, 138, 141, 162, 164, 166

N
national corpus/corpora, v, 2, 4, 6, 7, 17, 24, 25, 28, 46, 68, 87, 96, 108, 138, 166–168
non-dominant language, vi, 8, 9

P
(participant) recruitment, 61, 68, 76, 77, 150
permission/consent, 16, 61, 64, 65, 78, 81, 83, 95–97, 107, 121, 139, 141, 142, 150, 151, 156, 159, 162, 164–166
pilot, 60–63, 65, 83

Q
quality control (QC), 107, 110, 114, 139, 151, 152
query tools, 4, 14, 84, 99, 119, 123, 124, 126, 130, 131, 166

R
representative(ness), 6, 9, 24, 29, 32, 53, 61, 63, 77, 92, 93, 150

S
sample, 17, 24, 25, 29, 35, 40, 42, 47, 48, 52–54, 58, 59, 65, 80, 84, 94, 95, 114, 143, 148, 156, 159, 162
Spoken BNC2014, 30, 35, 37, 83, 87, 97, 108–110, 150, 152
spoken (corpora), 28–30, 47, 48, 83, 91, 107, 108, 112, 139

T
tag(set), 3, 99, 110, 111, 114, 118–120
taxonomy, 27, 28, 31–33, 36, 62, 143, 149, 152
token, 12, 13, 117, 118, 126, 138
transcription, 3, 4, 12–16, 83, 97, 106–115, 121, 123, 127, 139, 151, 152
transcription conventions, 84, 107–110, 112, 113, 117, 151

INDEX 183

transcription software, 111

U
under-resourced language, vi, 2, 4, 8–12, 14

W
well-resourced language, vi, 10, 18

Written BNC2014, 24, 48, 59–61, 79, 96, 157, 159
written (corpora), 13, 28, 46, 48, 54, 152

Y
ϒ *Tiwtiadur*, 99, 115, 130–132

CPSIA information can be obtained
at www.ICGtesting.com
Printed in the USA
LVHW080233161021
700534LV00003B/404